Lawyers' Practice & Procedure Series

Sheriff's Ordinary Court Practice & Procedure

by DB White, OBE

Formerly Sheriff Clerk, Edinburgh, and Regional Sheriff Clerk of Lothian and Borders

Second edition

Tolley Publishing Company Limited

A UNITED NEWSPAPERS PUBLICATION

ISBN 0 85459 864-2

First published 1988
Second edition 1994

Published by
Tolley Publishing Company Limited
Tolley House
2 Addiscombe Road
Croydon
Surrey
CR9 5AF
081-686 9141

© Tolley Publishing Company Limited 1994
Typeset in Great Britain by
Action Typesetting Limited, Northgate Street, Gloucester

Printed and bound in Great Britain by
Hobbs the Printers, Southampton

Preface to the first edition

Civil business in the sheriff court falls into several categories — ordinary causes (including divorce); summary causes; miscellaneous applications such as bankruptcy, adoption of children, registration of clubs etc; and commissary (probate) business. The bulk of civil business is dealt with in the Ordinary Court and the Summary Cause Court.

The Sheriff's Ordinary Court, although not the busiest in terms of volume, is the most important civil court in the sheriff court. The jurisdiction of the Sheriff's Ordinary Court is similar to that of the Outer House of the Court of Session, the main exceptions being actions relating to nullity of marriage, reduction, and proving the tenor of a document.

The Ordinary Cause Rules are contained in the Schedule to the Sheriff Courts (Scotland) Act 1907. The first major revision of the rules was enacted in 1983. Further amendments followed the introduction of divorce jurisdiction to the sheriff court, the implementation of the Civil Jurisdiction and Judgments Act 1982 and various family law statutes.

The following text deals with jurisdiction in the Sheriff's Ordinary Court, and the types of action raised in court; it also includes a commentary on the rules and the forms prescribed under the rules. All amendments to the rules and forms up to 1 September 1987 have been taken into account.

DBW
October 1987

Preface to the second edition

The Ordinary Cause Rules contained in the Schedule to the Sheriff Courts (Scotland) Act 1907 have been modified over the years, but the original concept was retained. The Sheriff Court Rules Council has carried out an extensive review of the Rules, the end result being the Act of Sederunt (Sheriff Court Ordinary Cause Rules) 1993, made by the Lord President on 29 July 1993 and which came into force on 1 January 1994.

The new Rules make fundamental changes to the procedure for dealing with a defended ordinary action, from raising the action to fixing a date for proof, the aim being to reduce the number of callings in court and to vest in the court the control and management of cases. Procedure in family actions, previously to be found in various Acts of Sederunt, is consolidated in the Rules as are procedures related to the Sex Discrimination Act 1975 and the Presumption of Death (Scotland) Act 1977.

A variety of forms are referred to throughout the text — these are reproduced in the Appendices.

DBW
January 1994

To the memory of OJB

Contents

Contents

Contents

Chapter 1

Jurisdiction

Jurisdiction in ordinary actions is based upon:

(i) the location of the pursuer or defender; and/or

(ii) the nature of the action,

and is regulated by various enactments.

The majority of ordinary actions are covered by the provisions of the Civil Jurisdiction and Judgments Act 1982 which largely replaced s 6 of the Sheriff Courts (Scotland) Act 1907. Certain types of action, mainly consistorial, are excluded from the provisions of the 1982 Act and are covered by other Acts including:

(i) the Domicile and Matrimonial Proceedings Act 1973;

(ii) the Law Reform (Parent and Child) (Scotland) Act 1986; and

(iii) the Family Law Act 1986.

The grounds of jurisdiction under the Civil Jurisdiction and Judgments Act 1982 are set out in Sch 8 of the Act and consist of:

(i) domicile;

(ii) special jurisdiction;

(iii) consumer contracts;

(iv) exclusive jurisdiction; and

(v) prorogation.

These are considered in turn below.

Domicile

Domicile is the principal ground of jurisdiction under the 1982 Act, which provides that 'persons shall be sued in the courts for the place where they are domiciled'. So far as ordinary actions are concerned, this will generally mean the sheriff court of the district in which the defender resides or carries on business.

Domicile is defined in the Act. In the case of an individual he is held to be domiciled in Scotland if:

(i) he is resident in Scotland; and

(ii) the nature and circumstance of the residence indicate that he has a substantial connection with Scotland.

1

So far as (ii) is concerned, residence in Scotland for three months is enough to indicate a substantial connection.

Having established that the individual defender is domiciled in Scotland, the action may be raised in the sheriff court of the sheriff court district in which he is resident.

In the case of corporations and associations, the seat of the corporation or association is treated as its domicile. The sheriff has jurisdiction over a corporation or association if:

(i)   it has its seat in the United Kingdom; and

(ii) it has its seat in Scotland; and

(iii) it has its seat in the sheriff court district.

A corporation has its seat in the United Kingdom if:

(i)   it was incorporated or formed under the law of a part of the United Kingdom and has its registered office or some other official address in the United Kingdom; or

(ii) its central management or control is exercised in the United Kingdom.

It has its seat in Scotland if:

(i)   it has its seat in the United Kingdom; and

(ii) it has its registered office or some other official address in Scotland; or

(iii) its central management or control, is exercised in Scotland; or

(iv) it has a place of business in Scotland.

It has its seat in the sheriffdom if:

(i)   it has its seat in Scotland; and

(ii) it has its registered office or some other official address in the sheriffdom; or

(iii) its central management or control is exercised in the sheriffdom; or

(iv) it has a place of business in the sheriffdom.

The location of the registered office, other official address or place of business determines the sheriff court in which the action may be raised.

Special jurisdiction

The following grounds of special jurisdiction are additional to those under domicile (above) but subject to jurisdiction over consumer contracts, exclusive jurisdiction and prorogation of jurisdiction (below).

(a) Contract

In matters relating to a contract the action may be raised in the sheriff court for the place of performance of the obligation in question. Where the action relates to non-payment of sums due under the contract, the action should be raised in the sheriff court in whose jurisdiction the sums ought to have been paid. Where the action relates to non-performance, the action should be raised in the sheriff court in whose jurisdiction performance ought to have been made.

(b) Delict or quasi-delict

In matters relating to delict or quasi-delict the action may be raised in the sheriff court in whose jurisdiction the harmful event occurred.

(c) Maintenance

Actions relating to maintenance, other than those ancillary to actions affecting status, may be raised in the sheriff court for the place in which the maintenance creditor is domiciled or habitually resident.

Actions relating to maintenance matters ancillary to proceedings concerning status may be raised in the sheriff court which has jurisdiction to entertain those proceedings.

(d) Branch, agency etc

Actions relating to a dispute arising out of the operations of a branch, agency or other establishment may be raised in the sheriff court for the place in which the branch, agency or other establishment is situated.

(e) Arrestment

This ground of special jurisdiction does not apply to defenders domiciled in member states of the European Union (including the United Kingdom) except Greece, Spain and Portugal. It applies to actions raised in the sheriff courts for the place where:

(i) any moveable property belonging to the defender has been arrested; or

(ii) any immoveable property in which he has any beneficial interest is situated.

(f) Moveable property

Actions to:

(i) arrest, declare or determine proprietory or possessory rights or rights in security in or over moveable property; or

(ii) obtain authority to dispose of moveable property

may be raised in the sheriff court for the place where the property is situated.

(g) Interdict

Actions for interdict may be raised in the sheriff court for the place where it is alleged that the wrong is likely to be committed.

(h) Secured debts

Actions concerning a debt secured over immoveable property may be raised in the sheriff court for the place where the property is situated.

(i) Decisions of companies etc

Actions which have as their object a decision of an organ of a company or other legal person or of an association may be brought in the sheriff court for the place where that company has its seat.

(j) More than one defender

A defender who is one of a number of defenders may be sued in the sheriff court for the place where any one of them is domiciled.

(k) Third party claims

A person may be sued as a third party in an action on a warranty or guarantee or any third party proceedings in the sheriff court hearing the original proceedings. However, this ground of jurisdiction does not apply if the sole purpose of raising the original action was to make the third party subject to the jurisdiction of the court and remove him from the jurisdiction of the court to which he would otherwise be subject.

(l) Counterclaim

A person may be sued on a counterclaim arising from the same contract or facts on which the original claim was based, in the sheriff court in which the original claim is pending.

Consumer contracts

This ground of jurisdiction is restricted to actions in which the contract was concluded by a person for a purpose which can be regarded as being outside his trade or profession. The following conditions have to be satisfied:

(i)   the contract has to be for the sale of goods on instalment credit terms; or

(ii) the contract has to be for a loan repayable by instalments or for any other form of credit made to finance the sale of goods; or

(iii) if, in any other contract for the supply of goods or services:

- the consumer took in Scotland the steps necessary for the conclusion of the contract; or

- the action is raised in the sheriff court for the place in which the consumer is domiciled.

The consumer has a choice of courts in which he may raise an action. It may be raised in:

(i) the court for the place in which the other party is domiciled; or

(ii) the court for the place in which he himself is domiciled; or

(iii) any court having jurisdiction as described in *(d)* or *(f)* above.

The other party may raise an action against the consumer only in:

(i) the court for the place where the consumer is domiciled, or

(ii) any court having jurisdiction as described in *(f)* above,

but has a right to bring a counterclaim in the court in which the original action in relation to the consumer contract is pending.

Parties may agree to prorogate the jurisdiction of the court, but only if:

(i) the agreement is entered into after the dispute has arisen; or

(ii) the consumer is allowed to raise the action in another court.

Exclusive jurisdiction

There are four types of action in which particular sheriff courts have exclusive jurisdiction and in which domicile or any other ground of jurisdiction do not apply:

(i) proceedings which have as their object rights *in rem* in, or tenancies of, immoveable property must be raised in the sheriff court for the place where the property is situated;

(ii) proceedings which have as their object the validity of the constitution, the nullity or the dissolution of companies or other legal persons or associations of natural or legal persons must be raised in the sheriff court of the sheriff court district in which the company, legal person or association has its seat;

(iii) proceedings which have as their object the validity of entries in public registers must be raised in the sheriff court of the sheriff court district in which the register is kept; and

(iv) proceedings concerned with the enforcement of judgments must be raised in the sheriff court of the sheriff court district in which the judgment has been or is to be enforced.

Prorogation of jurisdiction

The sheriff court which parties have agreed is to have jurisdiction to settle any disputes which have arisen or which may arise in connection with a particular legal relationship shall have exclusive jurisdiction except:

(i) where restrictions apply in relation to consumer contracts (see page 4);

(ii) where exclusive jurisdiction has been conferred on a sheriff court (see page 5).

Averments in the initial writ

Initial writs in actions to which the Civil Jurisdiction and Judgments Act 1982 applies must contain articles of condescendence stating:

(i) the domicile of the defender as determined in accordance with ss 41 to 46 of, and art 52 of Sch 1 to, the Civil Jurisdiction and Judgments Act 1982; and

(ii) the ground of jurisdiction of the court.

(see page 1).

The sheriff shall not grant decree in absence unless it appears *ex facie* of the initial writ that a ground of jurisdiction exists under the 1982 Act (see page 27).

Domicile and Matrimonial Proceedings Act 1973

Jurisdiction in actions for separation or divorce is governed by s 8 of the above Act which provides that an action may be raised in a sheriff court if:

(i) either party to the marriage in question is:
- domiciled in Scotland at the date when the action is begun, or
- was habitually resident there throughout the period of one year ending with that date; and

(ii) either party to the marriage:
- was resident in the sheriffdom for a period of forty days ending with that date; or
- had been resident in the sheriffdom for a period of not less than forty days ending not more than forty days before that date and has no known residence in Scotland at that date.

In practice, the action may be raised in the sheriff court of the sheriff court district in which the address of the party establishing jurisdiction is located.

Law Reform (Parent and Child) (Scotland) Act 1986

Section 7 of the above Act provides that an action for declarator of parentage, non-parentage, legitimacy, legitimation or illegitimacy may be brought in the sheriff court if:

(i) the child was born in the sheriffdom; or

(ii) the circumstances are such that the action could have been raised in the Court of Session and the alleged or presumed parent or the child was habitually resident in the sheriffdom on the date when the action is brought or on the date of his death.

Family Law Act 1986

Chapter 3 of Part I of this Act deals with jurisdiction of courts in Scotland in relation to child custody orders, otherwise than in matrimonial proceedings. The sheriff has jurisdiction to deal with such cases if, on the date of the application:

(i)   the child concerned is habitually resident in the sheriffdom; or

(ii) • the child is present in Scotland;
      • the child is not habitually resident in any part of the United Kingdom; and
      • either the pursuer or the defender is habitually resident in the sheriffdom.

The sheriff also has jurisdiction to deal with emergency applications where:

(i)   the child concerned is present in the sheriffdom on the date of the application; and

(ii) the sheriff considers that, for the protection of the child, it is necessary to make a custody order immediately.

Chapter 2

Classification of causes

Introduction

The term 'ordinary cause' (or 'ordinary action') is not defined in the Sheriff Courts (Scotland) Act 1907. Business in the sheriff's civil court is divided into the following categories:

   (i)   small claims;

   (ii) summary causes;

   (iii) summary applications; and

   (iv) ordinary causes.

In general, small claims procedure deals with actions of a monetary value not exceeding £750, and summary cause procedure deals with actions of a monetary value more than £750 but not exceeding £1,500. Guides to both procedures are available in sheriff clerk's offices.

Summary applications are defined, in s 3(p) of the 1907 Act, as:

> 'all applications of a summary nature brought under the common law jurisdiction of the Sheriff, and all applications, whether by appeal or otherwise, brought under any Act of Parliament which provides, or according to any practice in the Sheriff Court, which allows that the same shall be disposed of in a summary manner, but which does not more particularly define in what form the same shall be heard, tried and determined'.

All other actions are ordinary causes, the main classifications of which are described below, although this is not exhaustive.

Payment

Actions for payment are generally raised for the recovery of a debt for:

   (i)   goods supplied;

   (ii) services rendered; or

   (iii) money given under a loan or IOU.

Delict

Actions for delict (to remedy a legal wrong) may be classed under (a) damages or (b) reparation. The range is wide but includes the following actions:

(i) damages for:
- damage to goods in transit;
- infringement of copyright;
- breach of contract;
- trespass;
- failure to complete work; and

(ii) reparation for:
- wrongful arrest;
- breach of arrestment;
- assault;
- fraud;
- negligent performance of work;
- personal injury arising from road traffic accidents, medical treatment;
- breach of promise of marriage.

Family

Family actions deal with matters arising from family circumstances and relationships and include:

(i) divorce;
(ii) separation;
(iii) declarator of:
- legitimacy;
- illegitimacy;
- parentage;
- non-parentage;
- legitimation;
(iv) parental rights;
(v) affiliation and aliment;
(vi) financial provisions after divorce or annulment;
(vii) applications under the Matrimonial Homes (Family Protection) (Scotland) Act 1981;
(viii) variation or recall of Court of Session orders on aliment etc.

Accountancy

The most common action under this heading is one of count, reckoning and payment against a co-partner following dissolution of the partnership.

Contract

Actions under this heading include those for implement of or in respect of breach of contract.

Declarator

Apart from actions of declarator of marriage or nullity of marriage, which must be raised in the Court of Session, all other actions of declarator may be raised in the ordinary court. The range is wide but includes actions to find and declare that:

(i)   a will is holograph;

(ii) a right of way exists;

(iii) a building society has the right to enter into possession of heritable property; and

(iv) the pursuer has exclusive right to a trade mark.

Delivery

Actions for delivery normally relate to inanimate objects such as a purchased article, title deeds etc, but may also relate to delivery of a child. An action for delivery alone or an action for delivery combined with a crave for payment of a sum of money not exceeding £1,500 proceeds as a summary cause. An action for delivery combined with a crave for payment of a sum of money exceeding £1,500 proceeds as an ordinary action.

Division and sale of heritable property

Actions under this heading are often related to an action of divorce. Their purpose is to ask the sheriff to decide which portions of heritable property belong to joint proprietors and to authorise the sale of the property and the division of proceeds.

Actions of furthcoming

Moveable property belonging to a debtor may be arrested in the hands of a third party. If the debtor does not authorise the release of the property, an action of furthcoming is raised by the creditor.

Implement

An action of implement is a remedy when a party to a contract fails or refuses to fulfil an obligation under the contract.

An action for implement alone or for implement combined with a crave for payment of a sum of money not exceeding £1,500 proceeds as a summary cause. An action for implement combined with a crave for payment of a sum of money exceeding £1,500 proceeds as an ordinary action.

Interdict

An action of interdict may be raised in respect of an alleged wrong being committed or threatened to be committed and includes such matters as:

- access to premises;
- infringement of copyright;
- use of a trade name;
- trespass; and
- diversion of a water supply.

Multiplepoinding

An action of multiplepoinding may be raised when there are two or more competing claims on a fund *in medio* which may comprise moveable or heritable property. It may be raised by a claimant on the fund or by the holder of the fund. For example, if, following a criminal trial, there are competing claims to ownership of property held by the Procurator Fiscal, an action may be raised by one or more of the claimants, or the Procurator Fiscal may raise the action so that the sheriff may determine ownership.

Partnership

An ordinary action of declarator may be raised to find and declare that a partnership is at an end and should be dissolved.

Removing

The most common ordinary action of removing is that against a defender without a title, e.g. a squatter. An action of declarator of irritancy and removing may be raised by a superior against a vassal (see page 135).

Chapter 3

Citation, interpretation, representation and forms

The rules may be cited (referred to) as the Ordinary Cause Rules 1993. Normally, a party to an ordinary cause (or action) will be represented by a solicitor, but a party may conduct all stages of a litigation without legal representation. In proceedings arising solely under the provisions of the Debtors (Scotland) Act 1987, a party may be represented by a non-legally qualified person provided that the sheriff is satisfied that such person is a suitable representative and is authorised to represent that party; but this provision does not apply to an appeal to the sheriff principal.

The rules include a comprehensive list of forms in use in the Ordinary Court. The forms are referred to throughout the text, and are reproduced in the Appendix.

Chapter 4

Relief from compliance with the rules (r 2.1)

The Ordinary Cause Rules include directions to parties to carry out certain actions, sometimes within prescribed time limits. In some cases, the rules provide a specific remedy for the failure of a party to observe time limits. Where the rules do not so provide, the sheriff has a wide discretion to relieve any party from the consequences of failure to comply with the rules which is shown to be due to mistake, oversight or other excusable cause.

If the sheriff is satisfied that there was good reason for the failure, and that there was no wilful non-observance of the rules, he may exercise his dispensing powers on such terms and conditions as he considers just. The dispensing order specifies the action to be taken to bring procedure within the rules and, that having been done, the case proceeds as if the failure had not happened.

Chapter 5

Commencement of the case

Form of initial writ (r 3.1)

All ordinary causes are commenced by initial writ which is defined as:

'the statement of claim, petition, note of appeal or other document by which the action is initiated.'

(Sheriff Courts (Scotland) Act 1907 s 3(k)).

Its form must be as nearly as may be in accordance with Form G1 in the Appendix to the Ordinary Cause Rules (see page 159).

The rules provide for significant changes in lay-out of, and filing method for, the initial writ and any subsequent documents forming the process (case papers). In place of the previous system, whereby papers were folded lengthwise and tied in a bundle with tape, a flat process has been devised and all case papers will be retained in a pocket file.

The initial writ may be written, typed or printed on A4 size paper of durable quality; it need not be backed, and it must not be folded.

The initial writ must contain a statement, in numbered paragraphs, of the facts which form the grounds of the action. The statement is known as the condescendence. This requirement applies to all initial writs, but specific articles of condescendence are required in relation to jurisdiction in the following circumstances:

(i) *prorogation* — if the pursuer has reason to believe that an agreement may exist prorogating the jurisdiction over the subject matter of the cause to another court, the initial writ must contain an averment to that effect but there is no requirement to insert a negative averment;

(ii) *pending proceedings* — if the pursuer has reason to believe that proceedings may be pending before another court involving the same cause or action and between the same parties as those named in the initial writ, the initial writ must contain an averment to that effect, but there is no requirement to insert a negative averment.

An article of condescendence must be included stating the grounds of jurisdiction of the court and the facts on which the ground of jurisdiction is based.

In actions of divorce or of separation it is obligatory to insert an article of condescendence specifying whether any proceedings are continuing (i.e. not finally disposed of) in Scotland or elsewhere in respect of the marriage to which the initial writ relates. If there are proceedings which are continuing, the articles of condescendence must specify:

(i) the court, tribunal or authority before which they have been commenced;

(ii) the date of commencement;

(iii) the names of the parties;

(iv) whether a proof or hearing has been appointed and, if so, the date; and

(v) any other facts which might assist the sheriff to determine whether the action before him should be sisted in terms of Sch 3 to the Domicile and Matrimonial Proceedings Act 1973.

(Information about continuing proceedings, as mentioned above, must also be inserted in any defences or minutes lodged by any party if it is additional to or contradictory of the information provided by the pursuer, or if the pursuer has provided no such information.)

Applications under the Domicile and Matrimonial Proceedings Act 1973 by a party in an action of divorce or of separation:

(i) for an order under Sch 2 to the 1973 Act (such as interim aliment or regulating the custody of children); or

(ii) for a sist or recall of a sist under Sch 3 to the 1973 Act (because proceedings in respect of the marriage are proceeding in another jurisdiction),

must be made by written motion.

Where an initial writ in an action of divorce is presented to the sheriff clerk it must be accompanied by:

(i) an extract of the relevant entry in the register of marriages; and

(ii) where appropriate, an extract of the relevant entry in the register of births.

A warrant to cite will not be granted if the necessary documents are not presented, unless the sheriff, on cause shewn, otherwise directs.

In cases where the residence, registered office or place of business of the defender is not known and cannot reasonably be ascertained, the pursuer should include a statement to that effect in the condescendence and describe the steps which have been taken to ascertain the present whereabouts of the defender. For the method of citation of defenders whose address in not known, see rule 5.6 (page 23).

The initial writ must be signed by the pursuer or his solicitor. The name and address of the solicitor, if any, must be stated on the back of every service copy.

The requirements set out above apply to all initial writs except those in family actions the requirements for which are set out in r 33.2 (page 97).

Actions relating to heritable property (r 3.2)

In an action relating to heritable property, the holder of a heritable security over the property (for example, a building society which has granted a mortgage) need not be called as a defender unless:

(i)   the action relates to any heritable right or title; or

(ii) in any other case, where the sheriff so orders.

Warrants of citation (r 3.3)

When the initial writ has been presented to the sheriff clerk, the normal first procedure is for the grant of a warrant to cite the defender (to inform him that he is being sued and to provide him with a copy of the initial writ, the service copy).

The wording of the warrant of citation depends on the subject matter of the action.

Warrants to cite in:

(i)   family actions; and

(ii) actions of multiplepoinding

are dealt with in Chapters 35 and 37 respectively.

If the action is one in which the defender may apply for a time to pay direction under the Debtors (Scotland) Act 1987, the warrant of citation to be used is that in Form O2 in which case, in addition to a copy of the initial writ and warrant of citation, the defender must be served with a notice in Form O3.

In all other cases the warrant of citation to be used is that in Form O1.

Arrestment to found jurisdiction (r 3.4)

It may be necessary to execute an arrestment to found jurisdiction against the defender, i.e. arrestment of moveable property belonging to the defender, or immoveable property in which he has a beneficial interest, and located within the court's jurisdiction, for the purpose of giving the court jurisdiction over the defender (see page 3). In such a case, application may be made in the initial writ, but there must be averments in the condescendence to justify granting the warrant. This procedure is restricted to defenders who are domiciled furth of the United Kingdom and the European Union.

Warrants and precepts for arrestment on dependence (r 3.5)

The purpose of arrestment on the dependence of an action is to prevent the defender from disposing of part or all of his moveable property with the intention of preventing the pursuer from gaining access to the property in the event of a decree being granted in favour of the pursuer.

It is standard practice to include a crave for a warrant to arrest on the dependence in an initial writ which contains a pecuniary conclusion (other than expenses) and the warrant is included in the warrant to cite.

A pursuer or defender who wishes to arrest on the dependence, but has omitted to crave a warrant to arrest, may present the initial writ or defences to the sheriff clerk for a document known as a precept of arrestment to be issued. This procedure is also available for execution of an arrestment on a liquid document of debt, for example a bill, but precepts of arrestment are rare or unknown in practice.

Period of notice after citation (r 3.6)

In all ordinary actions there is a period of time, following citation and before the case is returned to court, in which the defender may consider his position, take legal advice etc. This is known as the period of notice. The length of the period varies depending on where the defender is resident or has a place of business. The periods are:

  (i) where the defender is resident or has a place of business within Europe, twenty-one days after the date of execution of service; or
  (ii) where the defender is resident or has a place of business outside Europe, forty-two days after the date of execution of service.

The above periods may be shortened or extended by the sheriff, on cause shown by the pursuer, but a minimum of two days' notice must be given.

In fairness to the defender, where the period of notice expires on a Saturday, Sunday, public or court holiday, the period of notice is deemed to expire on the first following day on which the sheriff clerk's office is open for civil court business.

Chapter 6

Caveats

The purpose of a caveat is to ensure that warning is given to the person making the application (the caveator) that the court is being asked to make an order, such as interim interdict, against the caveator. Having received notice that such an application has been made, the caveator has an opportunity to address the court and show cause why the order sought ought not to be made.

Orders against which caveats may be lodged (r 4.1)

A caveat may be lodged against —

(i) an interim interdict before the defender has lodged a notice of intention to defend; or

(ii) an interim order sought before the expiry of the period within which the defender could lodge a notice of intention to defend.

Form, lodging and renewal of caveats (r 4.2)

Caveats should be in Form G2, remain in force for one year, and may be renewed for a further year and yearly thereafter.

Where a caveat is in force, the sheriff clerk is required to notify the caveator in terms of the caveat. A hearing is arranged, and the sheriff makes such order as he thinks fit. Before making an order in the absence of the caveator, the sheriff has to be satisfied that all reasonable steps have been taken to afford the caveator an opportunity of being heard.

Chapter 7

Citation, service and intimation

Introduction

In most ordinary causes, the defender resides in Scotland and the standard method of service is by recorded delivery post by the pursuer's solicitor. Normally, it is only where postal service has failed, for example because there is no answer, that alternative methods are used. The pursuer's solicitor instructs a sheriff officer to effect service, either by delivering the service copy document personally or by leaving a copy with a responsible person; or, failing personal contact, by leaving or affixing the service copy at the address — sometimes known as 'keyhole citation'.

Special provisons relating to service apply in cases of divorce or separation where the defender is suffering from a mental disorder or his whereabouts are unknown, and in respect of persons resident outwith Scotland.

Signature of warrants (r 5.1)

In the majority of cases, warrants for citation of the defender or for arrestment on the dependence (of the action) are signed by the sheriff clerk or one of his deputes. However, the sheriff may sign any warrant, and only he may sign a warrant containing an order shortening or extending the period of notice.

The sheriff clerk will normally satisfy himself of the *prima facie* competence of the initial writ. If he is not satisfied, and declines to sign a warrant for citation, the initial writ may be presented to the sheriff for his consideration.

Form of citation and certificate (r 5.2)

(i) Citations in actions in which a time to pay direction may be applied for by the defender is made in Form O5 which is attached to:

- a copy of the initial writ (the service copy);
- a copy of the warrant of citation;
- a notice of intention to defend in Form O7;
- a notice in Form O3; and

when service has been effected, a certificate of citation in Form O6 is attached to the initial writ.

(ii) Citation in all other actions is made in Form O4 which is attached to:

- a copy of the initial writ (the service copy);
- a copy of the warrant of citation; and
- a notice of intention to defend in Form O7; and

when service has been effected, a certificate of citation in Form O6 is attached to the initial writ.

Postal service or intimation (r 5.3)

Postal citation or service is by far the most common mode in ordinary causes. Although it is competent to use registered post, the normal method is by recorded delivery, in which case it must be by first class mail.

When postal service is used, the period of notice starts to run on the day after the day of posting.

The following notice must be printed or written on the face of the envelope sent by post:

'This letter contains a citation to or intimation from ... Sheriff Court. If delivery of the letter cannot be made at the address shown it is to be returned immediately to The Sheriff Clerk, Sheriff Court, ...'.

The receipt issued by the Post Office must be attached to the certificate of citation.

Service within Scotland by sheriff officer (r 5.4)

In ordinary cause procedure, various documents may have to be served on persons connected with the cause. Any initial writ, decree, charge, warrant or other order or writ may be served by a sheriff officer on any person:

(i) personally; or
(ii) by leaving it in the hands of a resident at the person's dwelling place or an employee at the person's place of business.

If the officer is unsuccessful in effecting service by either of these methods he may, after making diligent inquiries, serve the document either:

(i) by depositing it in the dwelling place or place of business, via the letter box or by other lawful means; or
(ii) by affixing it to the door of the dwelling place or place of business,

and in these cases the officer must, as soon as possible afterwards, send a copy of the document by ordinary post to the address at which he thinks it most likely that the person may be found.

Where an officer effects service by letter box or by affixing, the certificate referred to under r 5.2 must contain a statement of the mode of service previously attempted, the circumstances which prevented such service, and a statement that a copy of the document was sent to the address at which the officer thinks it most likely that the person may be found.

Service on persons furth of Scotland (r 5.5)

The method of service on persons outwith Scotland depends on the residence or place of business or location of the persons. It also depends on whether or not a Convention on the service of documents exists between the United Kingdom and the country concerned. Sheriff clerks will advise on the existence of a Convention. See also page 1 on jurisdiction.

(a) Methods of service

Where a person has a known residence or place of business in:

- England;
- Wales;
- Northern Ireland;
- the Isle of Man;
- the Channel Islands; or
- any country with which the United Kingdom does not have a Convention providing for the service of writs,

service is effected by:

(i) personal service in accordance with the domestic law of the country concerned; or

(ii) postal service in Scotland by registered post.

Where a person is located in a country which is a party to the Hague Convention or the European Convention, i.e.:

- Belgium;
- Denmark;
- France;
- Luxembourg;
- Netherlands;
- West Germany; and
- Italy,

service may be effected by one of the following methods:

    (i) by the method prescribed by the internal law of the country;

    (ii) by requesting the Foreign Office to arrange service;

    (iii) where the law of the country permits, by postal service in Scotland by registered post; or

    (iv) where the law of the country permits, by the equivalent of a sheriff officer.

Where a person is located in a country with which the United Kingdom has a Convention on the service of writs, other than the Hague Convention or the European Convention, service may be effected by one of the methods approved in the Convention.

(b) Translation

If English is not an official language in the country in which service is to be effected, all documents to be served must be accompanied by a translation into the language of the country. The translation must be certified correct by the translator whose full name, address and qualifications must be included in a certificate lodged with the execution of citation or certificate of execution.

(c) Postal service

The procedure for postal service is similar to that for persons resident or carrying on business in Scotland (see page 20 above). Service may be effected by a solicitor or a sheriff officer. The covering envelope must bear the same wording as is specified in r 5.3(3) (see page 20); but also there must be a translation of the wording into the language of the country if appropriate.

(d) Foreign Office

Where service is to be effected through:

    (i) a central authority in the country; or

    (ii) a British Consular authority,

at the request of the Foreign Office, a copy of the writ and warrant with citation attached (and a translation), with a request for service to be effected, should be sent to the Secretary of State for Foreign and Commonwealth Affairs. A certificate of execution of service by the authority which has effected service must be obtained and lodged in process.

(e) Sheriff officer equivalent

Where service is to be effected by the equivalent of a sheriff officer, the pursuer, his solicitor or the sheriff officer must send to the official in the country a copy of the writ and warrant for service with citation attached (and a translation), with a request for service to be effected by delivery to the defender or his residence. A certificate of execution of service must be obtained and lodged in process.

(f) Personal service

Where personal service is effected, the pursuer must lodge a certificate by a person who is conversant with the law of the country concerned, stating that the form of service is in accordance with the law of the country concerned. Such a certificate is unnecessary if service has taken place in another part of the United Kingdom, the Channel Islands or the Isle of Man.

Service where address of person is not known (r 5.6)

In ordinary actions in which the defender's address is unknown, the sheriff must grant warrant to cite the defender:

(i) by publication of an advertisement in terms of Form G3 in the schedule to the rules, in a newspaper circulating in the area of the defender's last known address; or

(ii) by displaying a copy of the instance and crave of the initial writ, warrant of citation and a notice in terms of Form G4 in the schedule to the Rules, on the Walls of Court.

The period of notice (fixed by the sheriff) runs from the date of publication of the advertisement or display on the Walls of Court. The documents to be displayed on the Walls of Court and the service copy for the defender must be lodged with the sheriff clerk by the pursuer.

The following documents must be lodged with the sheriff clerk by the pursuer:

(i) a certified copy of the instance and crave of the initial writ and the warrant of citation (where display on the Walls of Court is required);

(ii) a service copy of the initial writ and a copy of the warrant of citation (for possible collection by the defender); and

(iii) where appropriate, a copy of the newspaper containing the advertisement as evidence of publication.

If, following citation by newspaper advertisement or display on the Walls of Court, and after the cause has commenced, the defender's address becomes known, the sheriff may review the procedure, allow the initial writ to be amended and make orders relating to re-service of the writ, intimation, expenses or transfer of the cause, as he thinks fit.

Persons carrying on business under a trading or descriptive name (r 5.7)

Any person or persons carrying on a business under a trading or descriptive name, may sue or be sued in such trading or descriptive name alone.

Any extract of a decree:

(i) pronounced in the sheriff court; or

(ii) proceeding upon any document recorded in the sheriff court books in which execution may competently proceed

against such person or persons, under such trading or descriptive name, is a valid warrant for diligence against such person or persons.

Service of any document to which this rule applies is made at any place of business or office at which such business is carried on in the sheriffdom of the sheriff court in which the cause is brought or, if there is no place of business in the sheriffdom, service may be effected at any place (including the place of business or office of the clerk or secretary of any company corporation or association or firm) where such business is carried on.

Endorsation unnecessary (r 5.8)

In Scotland, any initial writ, decree etc may be served outside the jurisdiction of the originating sheriff court without the need to obtain an endorsation by the sheriff court within whose jurisdiction the document is to be served; and it may be served by a sheriff officer of the originating court or of the sheriff court district within which it is to be executed.

Re-service (r 5.9)

If the sheriff is satisfied that service of an initial writ on the defender has not been properly carried out, he may order the initial writ to be re-served on such conditions as he thinks fit.

No objection to irregularities in citation, service or intimation (r 5.10)

Irregularities in service can be corrected by re-serving the initial writ but a party who appears in answer to the citation forfeits any right to challenge any irregularity in service. However, he is not barred from pleading that the court has no jurisdiction.

Chapter 8

Arrestment

Introduction

Arrestment is the procedure by which a creditor attaches moveable property belonging to the debtor but which is in the hands of a third party. It is executed by a sheriff officer serving a schedule of arrestment on the third party (the arrestee). The schedule may be served personally or by post.

Service of schedule of arrestment (r 6.1)

If a schedule of arrestment has not been served personally on an arrestee then:

   (i) in the case of an individual arrestee a copy of the schedule of arrestment must be sent by post (registered or recorded delivery) to:

- the last known place of residence of the arrestee; or
- if this is unknown, to the arrestee's principal place of business if known; or
- if this is unknown, to any known place of business; and

  (ii) in the case of a firm or corporation, the schedule must be sent by post (as above) to:

- the principal place of business, if known; or
- if this is unknown, to any known place of business.

In his execution of service of the arrestment, the sheriff officer must describe the method and specify the address to which the copy has been sent.

Arrestment on dependence before service (r 6.2)

If an arrestment on the dependence of an action is used prior to service, the action must be served within twenty days of the arrestment and, in undefended cases, decree in absence must be taken within twenty days of the expiry of the period of notice — otherwise the arrestment falls.

Where an arrestment on the dependence has been executed, the party using it must forthwith report the execution to the sheriff clerk.

Movement of arrested property (r 6.3)

In the event of a vessel or cargo being arrested, whether to found jurisdiction or on the dependence, any interested party may apply, by written motion, to the court for authority to move the vessel or cargo. If the court grants the application, it may make such further order as it thinks fit to give effect to the warrant authorising movement.

Chapter 9

Undefended causes

Introduction

As a general rule, if no notice of intention to defend has been lodged by the defender within the period of notice (see page 17), the pursuer's solicitor may endorse a minute on the initial writ asking the court to grant decree, without the need for the pursuer or his solicitor to appear in court; this procedure is known as granting decree in absence.

Exceptions to the general rule apply to:

(i) certain types of action in which the sheriff may not grant decree without evidence (see page 112);

(ii) cases in which an application for a time to pay direction has been lodged (see below); and

(iii) cases to which the Hague Convention applies (see below).

Minute for granting of decree without attendance (r 7.2)

If a notice of intention to defend has been lodged, the pursuer's solicitor will have been advised of this by the sheriff clerk (see r 9.2), and if no such advice is received from the sheriff clerk it is reasonable to assume that no notice of intention to defend has been lodged, in which case, if the case is not one in which an application for a time to pay direction may be applied for, the solicitor endorses a minute on the initial writ craving decree with expenses and delivers the writ to the sheriff clerk. The procedure thereafter depends on the domicile of the defender.

(a) Defender domiciled in Scotland

If the sheriff is satisfied that:

(i) no notice of intention to defend has been lodged;

(ii) the defender is domiciled in Scotland and a ground of jurisdiction exists under the Civil Jurisdiction and Judgments Act 1982 (the initial writ must contain averments to this effect — see r 3.1, page 14); and

(iii) the initial writ has been lawfully served and is accompanied by a certificate of citation,

decree is granted.

(b) Defender domiciled in another part of the United Kingdom or in another contracting state

If the sheriff is satisfied that the requirements set out in *(a)* above have been met and, in addition, that the defender has been able to receive the initial writ in sufficient time to arrange for his defence or that all necessary steps have been taken to that end, decree is granted.

Decree in causes to which the Hague Convention applies

In cases in which the initial writ has been served in a country to which the *Hague Convention on the Service Abroad of Judicial Documents* applies, before granting decree the sheriff must be satisfied that, *inter alia*, the following requirements have been met:

(i)   service has been effected in terms of r 5.5 (see above); or
(ii) service has been effected in a way which conforms to the following conditions:

•   the document was transmitted by one of the methods provided for in the Convention;
•   a period of not less than six months, as may be considered adequate by the sheriff, has elapsed since the date of transmission of the document; and
•   no certificate of any kind has been received, even though every reasonable effort has been made to obtain it through the competent authorities of the state addressed.

Applications for time to pay directions in undefended causes (r 7.3)

In cases in which a time to pay direction may be applied for (see page 16), the defender is advised (in Form O3) that he may apply for such a direction and, if he does so timeously, the pursuer's solicitor will be advised of the application when he checks with the sheriff clerk. Where the pursuer's solicitor does not object to the application, decree may be granted as described above. But if the pursuer's solicitor objects to the application, he may minute the initial writ for decree, after which the sheriff clerk fixes a date for a hearing on the defender's application and intimates the date to the pursuer and defender. The sheriff then gives a decision on the application, and he may do so whether or not any of the parties appear.

The procedure set out above applies equally to an application by the defender to have an arrestment recalled or restricted.

Decree for expenses (r 7.4)

It is normal when craving decree in absence to elect to charge the scale fee of expenses, and decree in terms of the crave and decree for expenses and outlays are granted together. However, if the pursuer elects to have expenses in the cause taxed by the auditor of court, a finding for expenses will be made, and decree for the amount of expenses will be granted at a later stage, i.e. when the auditor of court's report has been lodged and approved (see also page 95).

Finality of decree in absence (r 7.5)

A decree in absence may be challenged in the following ways:

(i) by reponing (see Chapter 10);

(ii) by raising an action, in the Court of Session, to have the decree suspended — the effect being that the execution of diligence on the decree is suspended until questions on the legal position have been determined.

In the absence of any challenge, the decree in absence becomes final and entitled to the privileges of a decree *in foro* (as in a case in which the defender has entered appearance) within six months of its date or the date of charge under it, provided that service of the initial writ or charge has been personal. In all other cases the decree in absence becomes final after twenty years from its date.

Section 9(7) of the Land Tenure Reform (Scotland) Act 1974 makes separate provisions for the finality of a decree granted under that Act.

Amendment of initial writ (r 7.6)

In an undefended action, the sheriff has the same power to allow amendment of the initial writ as he has in defended actions. The extent of the power is set out in r 18.2 (see page 53).

The need to request amendment normally arises after the initial writ has been served — and a defect has been identified in the designation of one or other of the parties, in which case the sheriff will normally allow amendment and order re-service of the writ. However, if the requested amendment is radical, e.g. substitution of one defender for another, the remedy may be to draw a new initial writ.

The defender will not be liable for expenses occasioned by the amendment, unless the sheriff otherwise directs.

If diligence, such as an arrestment on the dependence of the action (see Chapter 8), has been used before amendment of the initial writ, the amendment shall not have the effect of validating the diligence if this prejudices the rights of creditors of the debtor (who may be interested in defeating the diligence). But the amendment has the effect of obviating any objection by the defender, or any person representing him by a title, or in right of a debt contracted by him, subsequent to the execution of such diligence.

Chapter 10

Reponing (r 8.1)

Reponing is a form of appeal. It applies to all decrees in absence in ordinary actions with the exception of:

(i)   actions of divorce;
(ii) actions of separation;
(iii) actions relating to legitimacy and parentage; and
(iv) actions to which the Presumption of Death (Scotland) Act 1977 applies (see Chapter 39).

A reponing note may be lodged at any time before implementation in full of a decree in absence. Implementation in full depends on the circumstances. If the decree has been complied with, e.g. by payment to the pursuer of the sum decerned for, reponing is not appropriate but where only part of the sum decerned for has been paid, the defender can be reponed for the balance.

The defender lodges with the sheriff clerk a note setting out his proposed defence to the action and his explanation for his failure to enter appearance. A copy of the note must be served on the pursuer. The normal practice is to serve a copy notice, by post or by hand, on the pursuer's solicitor before the note is lodged with the sheriff clerk. A diet is then fixed for hearing the application. The diet is intimated by the defender to the pursuer.

The application is considered at the hearing fixed and normal practice is to allow the pursuer to be heard, if he so wishes. If the sheriff is satisfied with the defender's explanation, he may recall the decree, so far as not implemented, and the action then goes ahead as if the defender had entered appearance.

A reponing note, duly lodged and served on the pursuer operates as a sist of diligence — the execution of diligence is suspended but diligence already executed is not recalled.

The sheriff's decision recalling, or incidental to the recall of, a decree in absence is final and not subject to review, but a decision to refuse a reponing note is appealable to the Sheriff Principal or to the Court of Session (ss 27 and 28 of the 1907 Act).

Chapter 11

Defended causes

The original rules in the Sheriff Courts (Scotland) Act 1907 contained a procedural timetable to be followed from the point at which the defender lodged a notice of intention to defend the action.

The case was enrolled for tabling on the first ordinary court day after the expiry of the period of notice, and the usual first order was for written defences to be lodged within ten days and the case continued, for adjustment of written pleadings, for two weeks. One more continuation after the first was allowed, but any further continuation was subject to cause being shewn. In practice, numerous continuations on the adjustment roll were commonplace, leading to unproductive use of court time.

The rules applied equally to the most straightforward case and the most complex case, and made no allowance for the fact that the issues in the former were, in most cases, capable of being brought into sharp focus at an early stage whereas the issues in the latter might require more procedural time.

The Sheriff Court Rules Council has addressed the points referred to above, the result being a system whereby, firstly, the adjustment of written pleadings is carried out with no direct involvement of the court (thereby saving court time), and, secondly, when the case comes before the court, the issues will be clear and the sheriff will be able to decide if the case should be dealt with under the 'standard procedure' (the fast track for straightforward cases) or, if the issues are complex, under the 'additional procedure'. The main difference between the procedures is that the 'additional procedure' has more flexibility so far as the further adjustment of pleadings is concerned.

Chapter 12

Standard procedure in defended causes

Notice of intention to defend (r 9.1)

The warrant of citation (attached to the service copy initial writ) directs the defender, if he intends to defend the action or make any claim to lodge a notice of intention to defend by completing Form O7 (attached to the service copy initial writ) and lodging it with the sheriff clerk within the period of notice.

Failure to lodge the notice before the expiry of the period of notice might not be fatal. The defender could apply to the sheriff for an extension of the period by exercise of the dispensing powers of the sheriff under r 2.1 (see page 13).

Lodging a notice of intention to defend covers not only defence of the action on its merits but also a challenge of the jurisdiction of the court; it does not imply acceptance of the jurisdiction of the court.

Fixing date for Options Hearing (r 9.2)

When a notice of intention to defend has been lodged, the sheriff clerk must fix a date and time for an Options Hearing to be held on the first suitable ordinary court day occurring not sooner than ten weeks after the expiry of the period of notice. There is no end-limit for the hearing date, but it is reasonable to expect it to be in the 10–12 week period.

On fixing the date for the Options Hearing, the sheriff clerk sends a notice in Form G5 to all parties in the case, setting out:

(i)   the last date for lodging defences (fourteen days after the expiry of the period of notice);

(ii) the last date for adjustment of written pleadings (fourteen days before the date of the Options Hearing); and

(iii) the date of the Options Hearing,

and signs an interlocutor (a minute of proceedings) recording the above dates.

Fixing of the date for an Options Hearing does not affect the right of parties to make any incidental application to the court.

Return of the initial writ (r 9.3)

The pursuer's solicitor must return the initial writ, unbacked and unfolded but with the appropriate certificate of citation (see Chapter 7) attached, to the sheriff clerk within seven days after the expiry of the period of notice.

Lodging of pleadings before Options Hearing (r 9.4)

Normally, the Options Hearing will be the first time the defended cause will be called in court. However, in some cases, either party may want to have the case called in court before the Options Hearing as a matter of urgency, e.g. the defender may wish to have an arrestment on the dependence recalled. If a hearing is fixed before the Options Hearing, each party must lodge an up-to-date copy of his pleadings including adjustments, if any, not later than two days before the hearing.

Process folder (r 9.5)

The old-style process consisting of various items folded lengthwise and tied with cotton tape has been replaced by a folder system which is designed to provide easier access to papers. The folder is provided by the sheriff clerk when the notice of intention to defend is lodged, and consists of:

   (i)   interlocutor sheets;
   (ii) duplicate interlocutor sheets;
   (iii) a production file;
   (iv) a motion file; and
   (v) an inventory of process.

The initial writ, defences, production and all papers relevant to the action are also included in the folder.

Defences (r 9.6)

Just as the initial writ sets out the case for the pursuer, the written case for the defender is set out in the defences. The condescendence in the initial writ is in numbered paragraphs and the defences must be in the form of answers in corresponding paragraphs and, like the pursuer, the defender must append pleas-in-law. The result is that, by comparing one document with the other, it is possible to see the case for both parties.

The defender must lodge defences within fourteen days after the expiry of the period of notice, and it is normal practice to send a copy of the defences to the pursuer's solicitor.

In addition to written defences, the defender may lodge a counterclaim (see page 57).

Implied admissions (r 9.7)

Defences, when first lodged, must contain answers to the pursuer's condescendence but they may, and normally do, introduce new matter. This in turn must be answered by the pursuer who, in answering, may raise new matter which requires answer by the defender and so on. If a statement of fact made by one party is within the knowledge of the other party and not specifically denied by that other party, the latter is held as admitting the fact. As a precaution, answers to the other side's statements often contain the phrase 'not known and not admitted'.

Adjustment of pleadings (r 9.8)

The process of adjustment of pleadings under the old rules was subject to oversight by the court (the case was called in court on the adjustment roll when parties' solicitors would inform the sheriff of the latest state of play in the adjustment of pleadings). The new rules place the onus for the adjustment of pleadings on the parties' solicitors without any involvement of the court.

The period of adjustment begins when the defences are lodged (not later than fourteen days after the expiry of the period of notice) and ends fourteen days before the Options Hearing. This means that adjustment should be completed in a period of about 6−8 weeks, depending on the date fixed for the Options Hearing. No further adjustment will be permitted except with leave of the sheriff.

As stated above, the court is not involved in the adjustment process, and it is a matter for parties' solicitors to exchange adjustments and to maintain a record of adjustments made during the period of adjustment.

Effect of sist on adjustment (r 9.9)

Where procedure in a case has been sisted (suspended) with the authority of the court (e.g., to permit the defender to apply for legal aid), any period of adjustment before the sist is reckoned as part of the period for adjustment. On recall of the sist (by the court), the sheriff clerk:

  (i)   fixes a new date for the Options Hearing;
  (ii) prepares and signs an interlocutor recording that date; and
  (iii) intimates the date to each party.

In fixing the date, the sheriff clerk will take cognisance of any period for adjustment before procedure was sisted.

Open record (r 9.10)

When adjustment is complete, the record is closed and no further adjustment is permissible. This is a significant stage in procedure. The pleadings for both parties, as finally adjusted, are brought together in a single document known as the closed record (see r 9.12).

If the pleadings, original or as adjusted, are difficult to read together, being in separate documents for the pursuer and defender, the sheriff on his own motion or on the motion of a party may, at any time before closing the record, make an order for the pleadings to be brought together in a single document known as an open record, and, as the name implies, it is not as final as the closed record.

Record for the Options Hearing (r 9.11)

When the period for adjustment has ended (fourteen days before the Options Hearing), the pursuer's solicitor must bring together the written pleadings for both sides in a single document and lodge a copy, certified to be a true copy, with the sheriff clerk at least two days before the Options Hearing.

The Options Hearing (r 9.12)

The Options Hearing is the first occasion on which the case is called in court (apart from earlier incidental applications, if any). The sheriff is required to secure expeditious progress of the case by ascertaining from parties the matters in dispute and any other relevant information. Parties are required to provide the sheriff with such information as he may require.

The options available are:

(i) to close the record and fix a diet of:
- proof;
- proof before answer; or
- debate;

(ii) to order that the case proceed under additional procedure; or

(iii) to continue the Options Hearing.

If the sheriff is satisfied with the state of the pleadings and that there is nothing unduly complex and no preliminary pleas have been entered, the standard procedure is to close the record and fix a diet of proof. If preliminary pleas have been entered, and provided that a note of the basis of the plea has been lodged and intimated to the other parties, the sheriff may, having heard parties, fix a diet of proof before answer or debate (see page 63). In fixing a diet of proof or proof before answer, the sheriff may make such orders as to the extent of proof, the lodging of a joint minute of admissions or agreement, or such other matter as he thinks fit.

If the sheriff is satisfied that the difficulty or complexity of the case makes it unsuitable for the standard procedure, he may, on his own motion or on the motion of any party — and having given the parties the opportunity of being heard — order that the case proceed under the additional procedure (see page 37).

If the sheriff is satisfied that cause has been shown, he may, on his own motion or on the motion of any party, allow a continuation of the Options Hearing for a period not exceeding twenty-eight days or to the first suitable court day thereafter. The thrust of the procedure leading up to the Options Hearing is to encourage parties' solicitors to finalise adjustments to pleadings; hence, cause has to be shown before a continuation is allowed. During the continuation period, parties' solicitors may adjust pleadings until fourteen days before the date of the continued Options Hearing. If adjustments have been made during the continuation, a fresh certified copy record has to be prepared and lodged with the sheriff clerk not later than two days before the continued Options Hearing.

At the continued Options Hearing diet, the options available to the sheriff are those listed above save for further continuation, which is not permissible.

If any party in the case fails to appear or to be represented at the Options Hearing, that party shall be in default and the sheriff may grant decree as craved, decree of absolvitor, or dismiss the case, and make an award of expenses. If no party appears or is represented at the Options Hearing, the sheriff may dismiss the case.

Inspection and recovery of documents (r 9.13)

The purpose of this rule is to ensure that parties in the case are given reasonable notice of and access to documents which the other party or parties intend to use or put in evidence at the proof. Within fourteen days of the interlocutor allowing proof or proof before answer, each party must provide all other parties with a list of documents to be used or put in evidence, and give notice of the time and place where such documents may be inspected.

Documents not on the list may be used or put in evidence provided that there is no objection by any other party; if there is objection, leave of the sheriff must be sought.

Exchange of list of witnesses (r 9.14)

In the same way that notice of documents to be used has to be given, each party must provide all other parties with a list of witnesses to be called to give evidence. The list has to be intimated within fourteen days of the date of the interlocutor allowing a proof or proof before answer and, in the same way as applies to documents, a party who wishes to call as a witness a person not on the list may do so only if no other party objects and, if there is objection, leave of the sheriff must be sought.

Application for time to pay directions (r 9.15)

The procedure for applying for a time to pay direction or for the recall or restriction of an arrestment in an undefended cause is described above (page 28). In defended cases, application must be made by motion (see page 48) before the sheriff grants decree.

Chapter 13

Additional procedure

Introduction

This procedure applies to cases which the sheriff, at the Options Hearing, has decided are of either such complexity or difficulty to warrant more time for consideration of pleadings. The main difference between the standard procedure (described in Chapter 11) and the additional procedure is that the latter provides more time for the adjustment of pleadings.

Additional period for adjustment (r 10.1)

When, at the Options Hearing, the sheriff makes a direction that the case should proceed under additional procedure, the case is continued for adjustment for a period of eight weeks. The court is not involved in the adjustment process, and it is a matter for parties' solicitors to exchange adjustments and to maintain a record of adjustments made during the period of adjustment.

Effect of sist on adjustment period (r 10.2)

Where procedure in a case has been sisted during the adjustment period, the period of adjustment before the sist is reckoned as part of the overall period of adjustment.

Variation of adjustment period (r 10.3)

If the adjustment of pleadings has been completed before the expiry of the period of adjustment, it is open to parties, either jointly or by one with the consent of the other, to lodge a motion asking the sheriff to close the record without waiting for the adjustment period to expire.

On the other hand, and bearing in mind that the additional procedure applies to cases of complexity or difficulty, the sheriff may, if satisfied that there is sufficient reason for doing so, extend the period for such length of time as he thinks fit.

Any party may lodge a motion seeking an extension. He is required:

   (i)   to provide an up-to-date copy of the record as adjusted;

  (ii)   to give reasons for the request; and

 (iii) to specify the extension sought.

There is no limit to the number of motions for extension which may be lodged.

Order for open record (r 10.4)

At any time before the closing of the record, the sheriff may call for an open record to be lodged (see page 34).

Closing the record (r 10.5)

On the expiry of the period of adjustment the record is closed. This is a formal stage in the procedure. The sheriff clerk:

(i)   prepares and signs an interlocutor recording the closing of the record;

(ii) fixes a date for a Procedural Hearing — to be held on the first suitable court day not sooner than twenty-one days after the closing of the record; and

(iii) intimates the date of the hearing to each party.

Within fourteen days of the date of the interlocutor closing the record (which, normally, will be the first business day after the expiry of the period of adjustment), the pursuer's solicitor must lodge with the sheriff clerk a certified copy of the closed record which should contain only the pleadings of the parties.

Procedural Hearing (r 10.6)

The procedure at this hearing is similar to that at an Options Hearing, except that no provision is made for a continuation of the hearing.

The sheriff is required to secure expeditious progress of the case by ascertaining from parties the matters in dispute and any other relevant information. Parties are required to provide the sheriff with such information as he may require.

The normal procedure is to fix a diet of proof unless preliminary pleas have been entered, in which case parties' solicitors are given an opportunity of being heard on the pleas, after which the sheriff may fix a diet of debate or a proof before answer (see page 63).

In fixing a diet of proof or proof before answer, the sheriff may make such orders as to the extent of proof, the lodging of a joint minute of admissions or agreement, or such other matter as he thinks fit.

Chapter 14

The process

Introduction

The 1993 Rules change the format of the ordinary cause process from a bundle of documents folded lengthwise and held together with a piece of cotton tape or a rubber band to a single flat folder which holds all documents in the case and which is easier to handle and store. The folder is supplied by the sheriff clerk.

Form and lodging of parts of process (r 11.1)

All items of process must be on A4 size paper of durable quality; they must be lodged, unbacked and unfolded, with the sheriff clerk.

Custody of process (r 11.2)

Four items of process, namely:

   (i)   the initial writ;
   (ii) the interlocutor sheets;
   (iii) borrowing receipts; and
   (iv) the process folder,

remain in the custody of the sheriff clerk — however, the sheriff clerk may, on cause shown, authorise the initial writ to be borrowed by the pursuer, his solicitor or the solicitor's authorised clerk.

Borrowing and return of process (r 11.3)

Solicitors in the action may wish to examine the process, for example to adjust their pleadings. They can do so by visiting the sheriff clerk's office but, as a matter of convenience, they may borrow the process and work on it in their office. The process may be borrowed by the solicitor's authorised clerk, for whom the solicitor is responsible.

A party litigant cannot borrow a process except with leave of the sheriff subject to such conditions as the sheriff may impose. However, the party litigant is entitled to inspect the process in the sheriff clerk's office and, if practicable, to be supplied with copies of parts of the process.

A solicitor, having borrowed a process, is under an obligation to return it to the court within a reasonable time. If he delays and the other side is being denied access to the process, the sheriff clerk will ask him to return the process. If this is not effective, other remedies, such as process caption which could lead to imprisonment of the solicitor or his clerk, are technically available, although such remedies are unknown in practice.

Where a proof has been fixed, any parts of the process which have been borrowed must be returned not later than 12.30 pm on the day preceding the diet of proof (see page 86).

Failure to return parts of process (r 11.4)

The process must be present in court whenever the case is on the roll, so that it can be examined if necessary. Anyone who borrows a process or part of a process must return it in time for any calling at which it is required. Failure to do so renders that person liable to a fine not exceeding £50, payable to the sheriff clerk. The order imposing the fine may be recalled by the sheriff who granted it, on cause shown. There is no appeal against the sheriff's order.

Replacement of lost documents (r 11.5)

A copy of any item of process which has been lost or destroyed can be treated as if it were the original, provided the copy is authenticated as directed by the sheriff.

Intimation of parts of process and adjustments (r 11.6)

From the point where a notice of intention to defend is lodged, all parties are required to intimate to all other parties in the cause:

(i)   the lodging of a part of process; or

(ii) the making of an adjustment to pleadings,

and to send to all other parties a copy of each part of process of adjustment including, where practicable, copies of any documentary production. This is now a requirement, having been a matter of courtesy hitherto.

Various methods for transmitting documents to the other parties are available. Any of the methods of service described in Chapter 7 may be used, and it is advisable to use such a method where a degree of formality may be desirable, for example when dealing with a party litigant.

The normal methods where intimation is to a party represented by a solicitor are:

(i)   personal delivery;

(ii) facsimile transmission (fax);

(iii) first class ordinary post; or

(iv) delivery to a document exchange.

Intimation under methods (i) and (ii) above is deemed to have been given:

(i) on the day of transmission/delivery if made before 5 pm; or

(ii) on the day after transmission/delivery if made after 5 pm.

Intimation under methods (iii) and (iv) is deemed to have been given on the day after posting or delivery.

Any intimation given on a Saturday, Sunday, or public or court holiday is deemed to have been given on the next day on which the sheriff clerk's office is open for civil court business.

Retention and disposal of parts of process by the sheriff clerk (r 11.7)

Where a case has been finally determined, i.e. the subject matter has been disposed of and the matter of expenses has been dealt with and the period for marking an appeal has expired without an appeal having been marked, the sheriff clerk retains:

(i) the initial writ;

(ii) any closed record;

(iii) the interlocutor sheets;

(iv) any joint minute;

(v) any offer and acceptance of tender;

(vi) any report from a person of skill;

(vii) any affidavit; and

(viii) any extended shorthand notes of the proof,

and disposes of all other parts of process, except productions (see below).

If an appeal is lodged, the retention and disposal procedure is postponed until the final disposal of the appeal and any subsequent procedure.

Uplifting of productions from process (r 11.8)

Each party who has lodged productions is required to uplift the productions within fourteen days of the final determination where there is no appeal, or within fourteen days of the disposal of the appeal where one is marked, failing which the sheriff clerk intimates to the solicitor, party or such other person as seems appropriate that, if the productions are not uplifted within twenty-eight days, they will be disposed of in such manner as the sheriff directs.

Chapter 15

Interlocutors

Signature of interlocutors by the sheriff clerk (r 12.1)

This is an innovation and reflects the practice in the Court of Session whereby Clerks of Session are empowered to sign certain interlocutors. The Rules give discretion to the sheriff principal to prescribe a potentially wide range of interlocutors which may be signed by sheriff clerks in courts in the sheriffdom, the only exception being a final interlocutor, i.e. 'an interlocutor which, by itself, or taken along with previous interlocutors, disposes of the subject matter of the cause, notwithstanding that judgment may not have been pronounced on every question raised, and that expenses found due may not have been modified, taxed or decerned for' (1907 Act, s 3(h)).

Further provisions in relation to interlocutors (r 12.2)

The sheriff may sign an interlocutor when outwith his sheriffdom. Any clerical or incidental error in an interlocutor or note attached to it may be corrected at any time before extract.

In every case, other than an undefended family action, which proceeds to judgment, the sheriff issues an interlocutor setting out:

(i) findings in fact and law;

(ii) the decree or order;

(iii) a finding of liability for expenses (although these may not have been quantified); and

(iv) a note which gives the reasons for his decision.

The note is for the information of the parties in the case and also for any court dealing with a subsequent appeal. The sheriff may append a note to any other interlocutor, and must do so if requested by a party in the case.

When the sheriff has reserved his decision, the interlocutor — when written — is passed to the sheriff clerk who, upon the day of receipt, enters that date in the interlocutor and sends a copy interlocutor and any note attached free of charge to each party.

Chapter 16

Party minuter procedure

Introduction

Rule 20.1 (see page 59) provides for a defender applying by motion for an order for service of a third party notice on a person for the purpose of convening that person as a third party to the action. This procedure is restricted to an application by the defender so that any person with an interest and who has not been called as a defender or third party is prevented from using it, but a remedy is available under party minuter procedure.

Person claiming title and interest to enter process as defender (r 13.1)

A person who has not been called as a defender or third party may apply by minute for leave to enter a process as a party minuter and to lodge defences.

The minute must specify:

(i) the applicant's title and interest to enter the process; and

(ii) the grounds of the defence that he proposes to state.

An interlocutor:

(i) fixing a date and time for hearing the minute; and

(ii) authorising service on all parties in the action,

is pronounced. Service is made by one of the methods described in Chapter 7.

At the hearing the sheriff may:

(i) if he is satisfied that the applicant is entitled to enter the process, grant the applicant leave to enter the process as a party minuter and to lodge defences; and

(ii) make such order as to expenses or otherwise as he thinks fit,

but, if the application has been made after the closing of the record, the sheriff will only grant leave if he is satisfied as to the reason why earlier application was not made.

Procedure following leave to enter process (r 13.2)

When answers have been lodged by the party minuter, the sheriff clerk fixes a date for an Options Hearing on the first suitable court day occurring not sooner than ten weeks after the date for lodging answers.

At the Options Hearing, or at any time thereafter, the sheriff may grant such decree or other order as he thinks fit. A decree or other order against the party minuter has effect and is extractable in the same way as a decree or other order against a defender.

Chapter 17

Minutes and motions

Introduction

There is no clear-cut distinction between a minute and a motion. In general, a minute is appropriate where a fundamental change to the case or its conclusion is sought whereas a motion is appropriate as a procedural step in a depending action. The matter is further complicated by the fact that a motion may be made orally or lodged in writing. However, direction is given in individual rules as to whether application should be made by minute or motion.

This chapter does not deal with minutes of amendment (see page 54) or minutes of abandonment (see page 64).

Minutes

Form of minute (r 14.2)

A minute is similar in form to an initial writ and contains:

(i)   the names and designations of parties as in the initial writ;
(ii) a crave;
(iii) where appropriate, a condescendence in the form of a statement of facts supporting the crave; and
(iv) where appropriate, pleas-in-law.

Procedure in minutes (r 14.3)

Different procedures apply depending on whether the minute applies to a person who is a party to the action or not. If the minute seeks leave for a person:

(i)   to be sisted as a party to the action; or
(ii) to appear in the proceedings,

or for the cause to be transferred against the representatives of a party who has died or is under a legal incapacity, the party lodging the minute may ask for a date for an Options Hearing to be fixed.

If the minute is directed towards a party in the case, the minuter may seek leave for the lodging of answers within a period specified in the minute.

Lodging of minutes (r 15.1 as applied by r 14.1)

Any document referred to in the minute and not already lodged in process must be lodged with the minute. The sheriff clerk advises the minuter of the date, time and place of the hearing.

Intimation of minutes (r 15.2 as applied by r 14.3)

There is no requirement on a minuter to intimate the lodging of a minute to a person who is not, at that stage, a party to the action. If, after a hearing, the sheriff grants the crave of the minute, citation will be ordered.

In all other cases, the minuter is required to intimate the minute, with a copy of any document referred to in the minute, to every other party either by any of the methods of service described in Chapter 7, or, where intimation is to a party represented by a solicitor, by:

(i)   personal delivery;

(ii) facsimile transmission (fax);

(iii) first class ordinary post; or

(iv) delivery to a document exchange,

to that solicitor.

Intimation under methods (i) and (ii) is deemed to have been given:

(i)   on the day of transmission or delivery if made before 5 pm; or

(ii) on the day after transmission or delivery if made after 5 pm.

Intimation under methods (iii) and (iv) is deemed to have been given on the day after posting or delivery.

Any intimation given on a Saturday, Sunday, or public or court holiday is deemed to have been given on the next day on which the sheriff clerk's office is open for civil court business.

Intimation, where appropriate, must be made not less than seven days before the date fixed for the hearing of the minute, and a certificate of intimation in Form G8, with the necessary modifications, should be returned to the sheriff clerk not later than two days before the date fixed for the hearing of the minute; the sheriff may, on cause shown, dispense with or reduce the above time limits.

Opposition to minutes (r 15.3 as applied by r 14.3)

Any party seeking to oppose a minute must:

(i)   complete a notice of opposition in Form G9 (with the necessary modifications);

(ii) forthwith intimate a copy of that notice to every other party (by one of the methods described for intimation of minutes); and

(iii) lodge the notice with the sheriff clerk not later than two days before the date fixed for the hearing of the minute.

The sheriff may, on cause shown, dispense with or reduce the above time limits.

Hearing of minutes (r 15.4 as applied by r 14.3)

Minutes are dealt with by the sheriff or sheriff clerk depending on the circumstances.

If the minute is one:

(i) which the sheriff principal has authorised the sheriff clerk to deal with; and

(ii) in which no notice of opposition has been lodged,

the sheriff clerk may determine the minute; but if he considers that the minute should not be granted, he must refer the minute to the sheriff to be heard on the date fixed.

If the minute is one:

(i) being dealt with by the sheriff; and

(ii) in which no notice of opposition has been lodged,

the sheriff may determine the minute in chambers without the attendance of parties; but if a notice of opposition has been lodged, the minute must be heard in court on the date fixed.

Even though no notice of opposition has been lodged, the sheriff may require to be addressed by a party on the minute, in which case the sheriff clerk informs that party that the minute will be heard on the date fixed.

If the minute applies to a person who is not a party to the action (as described above), and is granted, the interlocutor will include a warrant to cite the person to whom the minute refers, in the same way in which a warrant to cite the defender is granted when an initial writ is lodged. However, unlike the normal initial procedure whereby an Options Hearing is fixed when a notice of intention to defend has been lodged, where the minuter has included in the crave of the minute a request for a date for an Options Hearing to be fixed, the interlocutor granting warrant to cite will include a date for an Options Hearing.

Motions

Lodging of motions (r 15.1)

A motion may be made orally, with leave of the court, on any occasion on which the case is in court for a hearing.

A motion may also be made by lodging a written motion in Form G6 together with any document referred to in the motion and not already lodged in process, unless this is not practicable. The sheriff clerk fixes a date for hearing of the motion, and intimates the date, time and place of the hearing to the party lodging the motion.

Intimation of motions (r 15.2)

The party lodging the motion is required to intimate the motion in Form G7, with a copy of any document referred to in the motion, to every other party, either by any of the methods described in Chapter 7 or, where intimation is to a party represented by a solicitor, by:

(i) personal delivery;

(ii) facsimile transmission (fax);

(iii) first class ordinary post; or

(iv) delivery to a document exchange,

to that solicitor.

Intimation under methods (i) and (ii) is deemed to have been given:

- on the day of transmission or delivery if made before 5 pm; or
- on the day after transmission or delivery if made after 5 pm.

Intimation under methods (iii) and (iv) is deemed to have been given on the day after posting or delivery.

Any intimation given on a Saturday, Sunday, or public or court holiday is deemed to have been given on the next day on which the sheriff clerk's office is open for civil court business.

Intimation must be made not less than seven days before the date fixed for the hearing of the motion, unless the rules require a longer period for intimation. A certificate of intimation in Form G8 should be returned to the sheriff clerk not later than two days before the date fixed for the hearing of the motion; the sheriff may, on cause shown, dispense with or reduce the above time limits.

Opposition to motions (r 15.3)

Any party seeking to oppose a motion must:

(i) complete a notice of opposition in Form G9;

(ii) forthwith intimate a copy of that notice to every other party (by one of the methods described for intimation of motions); and

(iii) lodge the notice with the sheriff clerk not later than two days before the date fixed for the hearing of the motion.

The sheriff may, on cause shown, dispense with or reduce the above time limits.

Hearing of motions (r 15.4)

Motions are dealt with by the sheriff or sheriff clerk depending on the circumstances.

If the motion is one:

(i) which the sheriff principal has authorised the sheriff clerk to deal with; and

(ii) in which no notice of opposition has been lodged,

the sheriff clerk may determine the motion; but if he considers that the motion should not be granted, he must refer the motion to the sheriff to be heard on the date fixed.

If the motion is one:

(i) being dealt with by the sheriff; and

(ii) in which no notice of opposition has been lodged,

the sheriff may determine the motion in chambers without the attendance of parties; but if a notice of opposition has been lodged, the motion must be heard in court on the date fixed.

Even though no notice of opposition has been lodged, the sheriff may require to be addressed by one or more parties on the motion, in which case the sheriff clerk informs the party who lodged the motion that the motion will be heard on the date fixed.

Chapter 18

Decrees by default (r 16.2)

The progress of a defended ordinary action depends on action being taken by one side or the other or both. The exception to this is where procedure has been sisted, e.g. to allow the defender to apply for legal aid. If one side fails to take action required of him, the other side may be entitled to decree — known as decree by default. The circumstances in which a decree by default may be granted are:

(i)   failure to lodge any production or pleading;

(ii) failure to implement an order of the sheriff within the time required; or

(iii) failure to appear or to be represented at a diet,

in which cases the sheriff may grant decree as craved if the default has been by the defender, or decree of absolvitor or dismissal if the default has been by the pursuer, with expenses to the successful party. These decrees are at the discretion of the sheriff who may, on cause shown, extend the time for lodging any production or pleading or for implementing any order.

If none of the parties appears at a diet, the sheriff may dismiss the cause. No decree is granted nor is there an award of expenses.

Decree by default procedure does not apply to:

(i)   family actions (see page 115);

(ii) actions of multiplepoinding (see Chapter 37); or

(iii) actions under the Presumption of Death (Scotland) Act 1977 (see Chapter 39).

Chapter 19

Summary decrees

Introduction

It is open to any party to state one or more preliminary pleas (see page 63) which, if sustained, would bring proceedings to an end. Such pleas are considered by the sheriff at the Options Hearing. Where any party considers that the written pleadings of any other party do not justify the action proceeding further, he may ask the sheriff to call a halt without further ado, and to grant summary decree. Application may be made at any time after defences or answers have been lodged, i.e. without waiting until the Options Hearing.

The procedure is not available in:

(i)   family actions;

(ii) actions of multiplepoinding; or

(iii) actions raised under the Presumption of Death (Scotland) Act 1977.

Applications for summary decree (r 17.2)

This rule applies to applications by the pursuer who may, at any time after defences have been lodged, apply, by motion, for summary decree against the defender on the ground that there is no defence to the action, or part of it, disclosed in the defences.

There are various options open to the pursuer. He may move the sheriff:

(i)   to grant decree in terms of all or any of the craves in the initial writ;

(ii) to pronounce an interlocutor sustaining or repelling a plea-in-law; or

(iii) to dispose of the whole or part of the subject matter of the cause.

The motion should be in Form G6 and lodged with the sheriff clerk who will fix a hearing of the motion, and will advise the party lodging the motion of the date, time and place of the hearing.

The procedure under this rule differs from the standard motion procedure in the following ways:

(i)   the pursuer must intimate the motion by registered post or first class recorded delivery service to every other party; and

(ii) intimation must be made not less than fourteen days before the date fixed for the hearing.

Although no provision is made for doing so, it would be prudent to serve a Form G7 with a copy of Form G6 (particularly if the party on whom service is being made is not legally represented). A notice of opposition (if any) should be lodged with the sheriff clerk not later than two days before the date fixed for the hearing.

A certificate of intimation in Form G8 should be completed and lodged with the sheriff clerk.

If no notice of opposition has been lodged, the sheriff may deal with the motion in chambers but, if the motion is opposed, it will be dealt with in court.

The options available to the sheriff are:

(i) if satisfied that there is no defence to the action or any part of it to which the motion relates, to grant summary decree in whole or in part;

(ii) to order any party, or a partner, director, officer or office bearer of any party:

- to produce any relevant document or article; or
- to lodge an affidavit in support of any assertion of fact made in the pleadings or at the hearing of the motion; or

(iii) to refuse all or part of the motion.

If the motion is refused, in whole or in part, a subsequent motion may be made where there has been a change of circumstances.

Applications of summary decrees to counterclaims etc (r 17.3)

Where a defender has lodged a counterclaim (see page 57) and is of the opinion that the answers to the counterclaim (lodged by the pursuer) do not constitute a defence to the counterclaim, or part of it, the defender may invoke the summary decree procedure as described above.

Where a defender or third party has made a claim against another defender or third party who has lodged defences or answers, as the case may be, and the defender or third party is of the opinion that such defences or answers do not constitute a defence to the claim, the defender or third party may invoke the summary decree procedure as described above.

Chapter 20

Amendment of pleadings

Alteration of sum sued for (r 18.1)

Adjustment of the initial writ or defences is restricted to condescendence, answers and pleas-in-law. Alteration of the crave is classed as an amendment and requires the permission of the sheriff. The exception to this rule applies to alteration of the sum sued for. This amendment, which must be made on the initial writ, the certified copy initial writ and the open record (if any) is competent in a case in which all other parties have lodged defences or answers, and the record has not been closed. The pursuer must intimate the amendment in writing to all other parties.

Powers of the sheriff to allow amendment (r 18.2)

The sheriff has power to allow amendment of the pleadings at any time before final judgment. With the exception of an amendment which alters the sum sued for, which may be done without leave before the record is closed (see r 18.1), all amendments require the leave of the sheriff.

One of the main considerations of the sheriff is to ensure that the issue between the parties is in sharp focus. If the sheriff decides that fundamental amendment of the initial writ is necessary, he may allow amendment even though this may result in:

(i)   the sum sued for being increased or restricted after the closing of the record; and/or

(ii) a different remedy from that originally craved being sought.

Amendment is often necessary to cure an error or omission which has been identified during the course of the action. Such amendments may be necessary:

(i)   to correct or supplement the designation of a party;

(ii) to enable a party who has sued or has been sued in his own right, to sue or be sued in a representative capacity;

(iii) to enable a party who has sued or has been sued in a representative capacity, to sue or be sued in his own right or in a different representative capacity;

(iv) to add the name of an additional pursuer whose concurrence is necessary;

(v) where the action has been commenced or presented in the name of the wrong person or it is doubtful whether it has been commenced or presented in the name of the right person, to allow any other person to be sisted in substitution for, or in addition to, the original person; or

(vi) to direct a crave against a third party brought into the action under third party procedure (see page 59).

In addition to amendment of the initial writ, referred to above, the sheriff may allow amendment of the condescendence, defences, answers, pleas-in-law or other pleadings which he considers necessary for determining the real question in controversy between the parties.

If it appears that all parties having an interest have not been called or that the action has been directed against the wrong person, the initial writ may be amended by the insertion of an additional or substitute party and by directing existing or additional craves, averments and pleas-in-law against that party.

Applications to amend (r 18.3)

Application is made by lodging a minute of amendment, setting out the proposed amendment accompanied by a written motion moving the court:

(i) to allow the minute of amendment to be received; and

(ii) to allow amendment in terms of the minute and, where appropriate, to grant an order for service on an additional or substitute party; and

(iii) if the minute is such that written answers may be required, to allow any other person to lodge answers within a specified period.

The minute of amendment and motion are lodged with the sheriff clerk who fixes a diet for a hearing and advises the party lodging the motion of the date, time and place of the hearing. Thereafter, the standard procedure for dealing with motions (see page 48) is followed.

Where the sheriff (or the sheriff clerk, as the case may be) has allowed the minute of amendment to be received, and has decided that written answers may be lodged, he may allow a period for adjustment of the minute and answers and, at the same time, fix a date for parties to be heard on the minute and answers as adjusted.

Applications for diligence on amendment (r 18.4)

Where a minute of amendment seeks to have a substitute or additional party brought into the action, the minuter may wish to execute diligence against the defender, e.g. by arrestment on the dependence, when the initial writ is first lodged (see page 16), and, if so, the minuter should lodge a written motion (in addition to the minute of amendment and written motion referred to above) moving the sheriff for warrant to use any form of diligence which could be used on the dependence of a separate action.

Arrestments on the dependence are normally executed without delay and without giving notice to the defender, and, for that reason, the standard motion procedure is inappropriate. The motion to authorise diligence is dealt with summarily and, if granted, a copy, certified by the sheriff clerk, of the interlocutor granting warrant for diligence on the dependence is sufficient warrant for the execution of diligence.

Service of amended pleadings (r 18.5)

Where a minute of amendment seeks to have a substitute or additional party brought into the action, and the motion accompanying the minute is granted, the party so brought into the action is in the same position as an original defender, and service of the amended pleadings is carried out in the same manner as for an original defender.

A copy of the initial writ or record (if any), as amended, is served by the party who made the amendment, on the substitute or additional party by one of the methods available for the citation of a defender (see Chapter 7). In a case in which a time to pay direction may be applied for, the service copy is served with Forms O3, O7 and O8, and in all other cases with Forms O7 and O9. The party who made the amendment must lodge in process:

(i) a copy of the writ or record as amended;

(ii) a copy of the notice sent in Form O8 or Form O9 as the case may be; and

(iii) a certificate of service in Form O6.

Thereafter, the action proceeds in every respect as if the substitute or additional party had originally been made a party to the action and, if a notice of intention to defend is lodged by such party, the sheriff clerk fixes a date and time for an Options Hearing in the usual way.

Expenses and conditions of amendment (r 18.6)

The party making the amendment will normally be found liable in the expenses occasioned by the amendment unless the sheriff is satisfied that it is just and equitable to find otherwise. The sheriff may attach such other conditions as he thinks fit.

Effect of amendment on diligence (r 18.7)

No amendment can have the effect of validating diligence on the dependence of an action, used prior to the amendment being allowed, in such a way as to prejudice the rights of creditors, of the party against whom the diligence has been executed, who are interested in defeating such diligence. But the amendment has the effect of precluding objections to such diligence by the party himself or by any person representing him by a title acquired or in right of a debt contracted by him subsequent to the execution of such diligence.

Preliminary pleas inserted on amendment (r 18.8)

Where a party seeks to add a preliminary plea (see page 63):

(i) by a minute of amendment;

(ii) in answers to a minute of amendment; or

(iii) by adjustment of the minute or answers as the case may be,

he must, at the time of lodging the minute, answers or adjustment, lodge a note of the basis of the plea, failing which he will be deemed to be no longer insisting on the plea which will be repelled by the sheriff.

Chapter 21

Counterclaims

Introduction

The practice whereby a counterclaim was stated separately from the defences has been changed. A counterclaim is now stated as part of the defences so that all pleadings for the defender are contained in a single document.

Proceeding by way of a counterclaim is an optional procedure and, if the subject matter is complex, it might be preferable to raise a separate counter-action.

Counterclaims (r 19.1)

A counterclaim may be lodged in any action other than:

(i) a family action; or
(ii) an action of multiplepoinding.

Certain conditions must be satisfied:

(i) the counterclaim must be such that it could have been made in a separate action in which it would not have been necessary to call as defender any person other than the pursuer; and
(ii) a counterclaim may be made in respect of any matter:
- forming part, or arising out of the grounds, of the action by the pursuer;
- the decision of which is necessary for the determination of the question in controversy between the parties; or
- which might have been the subject matter of an action against the pursuer in which jurisdiction would have been founded by reconvention. (A person not otherwise subject to the jurisdiction of the Scottish courts, renders himself liable to be sued in the sheriff court if he himself raises an action in that court.)

A counterclaim is incorporated in the defences:

(i) when the defences are lodged or during the period of adjustment; or
(ii) by amendment of the defences at any other stage, with leave of the sheriff and subject to such conditions, if any, as to expenses or otherwise' as the sheriff thinks fit.

Defences which contain a counterclaim are akin to an initial writ raised against the pursuer; they must be set out in similar form and should contain:

(i) a crave setting out the counterclaim;

(ii) answers to the condescendence of the initial writ (see page 33);

(iii) a statement of facts in numbered paragraphs setting out the facts on which the counterclaim is founded, with reference, if necessary, to any matter contained in the defences; and

(iv) appropriate pleas-in-law.

Warrants for diligence on counterclaims (r 19.2)

A counterclaim is similar to a substantive action raised by the defender against the pursuer, and the defender has similar rights to the pursuer so far as arrestment on the dependence is concerned (see page 16). Application by the defender for warrant to arrest on the dependence may be made:

(i) when lodging the counterclaim with the sheriff clerk, by inserting after the crave of the counterclaim the words 'Warrant for arrestment on the dependence applied for'; or

(ii) after the counterclaim has been made, for a precept of arrestment (see page 16).

It may be granted by the sheriff clerk writing on the defences or minute of amendment, as the case may be, the words 'Warrant granted as craved' (in which case the warrant has the same effect as if it had been in an initial writ) or by the issue of a precept of arrestment.

Effect of abandonment of cause (r 19.3)

The fact that a counterclaim has been lodged does not affect the pursuer's right to abandon his case, but any expenses awarded against the pursuer in connection with the abandonment will be separate from expenses of the counterclaim which may continue as a separate action.

Disposal of counterclaims (r 19.4)

The sheriff may:

(i) deal with a counterclaim as if it had been stated in a separate action;

(ii) regulate procedure as he thinks fit; and

(iii) grant decree in whole or in part or for the difference between the counterclaim and the sum sued for by the pursuer.

Chapter 22

Third party procedure

Applications for third party notice (r 20.1)

Third party procedure is appropriate if the defender claims that:

(i) he has a right of contribution, relief or indemnity against a person who is not a party to the action, such as the right of an insured person against an insurer; or

(ii) a person whom the pursuer is not bound to call as a defender is:

- liable with the defender to the pursuer in respect of the subject matter of the action, for example where, in an action of reparation for personal injury, the defender claims that a third party was wholly or partly to blame; or

- liable to the defender in respect of a claim arising from or in connection with the liability, if any, of the defender to the pursuer,

in which case the defender may apply by motion for an order for service of a third party notice in Form O10 to convene such person as a third party in the action. The procedure is not restricted to the defender. The third party, if convened, or a pursuer faced with a counterclaim by a defender may also use the procedure.

Averments where order for service of third party notice is sought (r 20.2)

If the defender intends applying for an order of service of a notice:

(i) before the closing of the record, he must state in his defences, by adjustment or in a separate statement of facts, averments setting out the grounds of the application and appropriate pleas-in-law; or

(ii) after the closing of the record, he must lodge a minute of amendment containing the averments and pleas-in-law referred to above, unless they have been set out in the defences in the closed record.

In either case, the defender must lodge a written motion not later than the commencement of the hearing of the action on its merits.

Warrants for diligence on a third party notice (r 20.3)

Application for a third party notice is similar to lodging an initial writ. Application for a warrant to arrest to found jurisdiction or for arrestment on the dependence is available in the same way as it is for an initial writ.

Averments in support of the application should be included in the defences or separate statement of facts, as the case may be, and application may be made by motion:

(i)   at the time of applying for the third party notice; or

(ii) if not applied for at that time, at any stage thereafter.

The application follows the standard motion procedure and, if the motion is granted, a certified copy of the interlocutor granting warrant is sufficient authority for execution of diligence.

Service on the third party (r 20.4)

The interlocutor granting the motion:

(i)   allows service of a third party notice on the third party; and

(ii) specifies twenty-eight days, or such other period as the sheriff on cause shown may specify, as the period within which the third party may lodge answers.

Service must be made within fourteen days of the date of the interlocutor — otherwise a fresh application must be made — using one of the methods available for the citation of a defender (see Chapter 7).

The documents to be served on the third party are:

(i)   a copy of:

• the pleadings (including any adjustment or amendment); or
• the closed record,
as the case may be; and

(ii) a third party notice in Form O10.

A copy of the notice, with a certificate of service attached to it, must be lodged in process by the defender.

Answers to a third party notice (r 20.5)

If the third party does not lodge answers within the period specified in the notice, the sheriff, having given the other parties an opportunity of being heard, may grant such decree or other order as he thinks fit.

If the third party decides to lodge answers, he must do so within the period specified in the notice.

Answers for a third party are the equivalent of defences, and should relate directly to the document to which they refer, namely:

(i)   the defences;

    (ii) a separate statement of fact; or

    (iii) a minute of amendment,

depending on how the defender set out his application for service of a notice.

If application was made in the defences, answers should be set out in numbered paragraphs corresponding to the numbered articles of condescendence in the initial writ. The third party's answers should relate to the defender's averments against him but, if he so wishes, he may incorporate answers to the pursuer's averments.

If the defender's application was in a separate statement of facts or a minute of amendment, the answers should be set out in numbered paragraphs corresponding to the numbered paragraphs of the statement of facts or minute of amendment, as the case may be.

In all cases, appropriate pleas-in-law should be included.

Procedure following answers (r 20.6)

Where the third party lodges answers, the sheriff clerk fixes a date and time for an Options Hearing being on the first suitable court day occurring not sooner than ten weeks after the date for lodging answers.

At the Options Hearing, or at any time thereafter, the sheriff may grant decree or such other order against the third party as he thinks fit, and such a decree or order has the same effect as a decree against a defender.

Chapter 23

Documents founded on or adopted in pleadings

Lodging documents founded on or adopted (r 21.1)

The principle on which this rule is based is that if a document is founded on by a party, or adopted as incorporated, in his pleadings, the document should be lodged in process without delay. This saves time and trouble. If necessary, the sheriff may order production of a document or grant diligence for recovery of it (see page 72).

The time for lodging a document founded on or adopted in:

(i) an initial writ is when the writ is returned after the expiry of the period of notice;

(ii) a minute, defences, counterclaim or answers is at the time of lodging that part of process; and

(iii) an adjustment to any pleadings is when such adjustment is intimated to any other party.

Consequences of failure to lodge documents founded on or adopted (r 21.2)

If a party fails to lodge a document on time, he may be found liable in the expenses of any order, for production or recovery of it, obtained by any other party.

Objection to documents founded on (r 21.3)

Normally a challenge of a deed or writing, such as to its validity, requires an action of reduction to be raised. Such an action is incompetent in the sheriff court and must be raised in the Court of Session. Objections to a deed or writing founded on by any party in an ordinary action may be taken by way of exception without the need to raise an action of reduction. Where such an objection is taken, and an action of reduction would be competent, the sheriff may order the objector to find caution or to give such other security as the sheriff thinks fit.

Chapter 24

Preliminary pleas

Introduction

A preliminary plea is a plea-in-law, by the pursuer, defender or third party, which, if sustained by the sheriff, will render it unnecessary to consider, in whole or in part, the merits of the action.

The most common types of preliminary pleas are normally directed against:

(i) the competency of the action, e.g. 'The pursuer has no title to sue the defender'; or

(ii) the relevancy of the pleadings, e.g. 'The defences are irrelevant and lacking in specification'.

Note of basis of preliminary plea (r 22.1)

A preliminary plea may be inserted as a plea-in-law in the initial writ, defences, counterclaim or answers by a third party, as the case may be, but if the party inserting the plea intends to insist on it, he must, not later than three days before the Options Hearing, or the Procedural Hearing under additional procedure:

(i) lodge in process a note of the basis of the plea; and

(ii) intimate a copy of the note to every other party.

If he fails to do either or both, he will be deemed to be no longer insisting on his preliminary plea, and the plea will be repelled by the sheriff at the hearing.

If, at the Options Hearing or Procedural Hearing, a preliminary plea is insisted on, and having heard parties and considered the note of the basis of the plea, and being satisfied that:

(i) it is necessary to hear evidence in the case before dealing with the preliminary plea, the sheriff may fix a diet for a proof before answer; or

(ii) there is a preliminary matter of law which justifies it, he may fix a diet of debate.

At any proof before answer or debate, parties may raise matters in addition to those set out in the note referred to above.

Chapter 25

Abandonment

Abandonment of causes (r 23.1)

The pursuer may abandon his case at any time before decree of absolvitor or dismissal has been granted. The main consideration from the defender's point of view is whether the decree is one of absolvitor, in which case the action is brought to a final conclusion and cannot be raised again, or one of dismissal, in which case the action can be raised again.

The pursuer lodges a minute of abandonment either:

   (i)   consenting to a decree of absolvitor; or

   (ii) seeking a decree of dismissal.

If the pursuer consents to a decree of absolvitor, the sheriff grants the decree and finds the pursuer liable in expenses.

If the pursuer seeks a decree of dismissal, the sheriff finds the pursuer liable to the defender, and any third party against whom he has directed a crave, in judicial expenses. The defender, and third party if appropriate, make up an account of expenses for taxation by the Auditor of Court (see page 95), and if the pursuer pays the taxed amount of expenses to the defender and, if appropriate, to a third party, within twenty-eight days of the taxation, decree of dismissal is granted. If the pursuer fails to pay on time, the defender, or third party, is entitled to a decree of absolvitor with expenses.

Application of abandonment to counterclaims (r 23.2)

A similar procedure applies to a defender who wishes to abandon his counterclaim.

Chapter 26

Withdrawal of solicitors

Intimation of withdrawal to court (r 24.1)

There are various reasons why a solicitor may decide to withdraw from acting on behalf of a party, e.g. there may be difficulty in obtaining instructions from the party, in which case he must intimate his withdrawal by letter to the sheriff clerk and to every other party. The letter to the sheriff clerk is lodged in process.

Intimation to party where solicitor has withdrawn (r 24.2)

The party whose solicitor has intimated his withdrawal may be aware of the position before the court is informed, but formal notice from the court is given to enable the party to continue the litigation either by himself or by instructing another solicitor.

The sheriff, on his own motion or on the motion of any other party, pronounces an interlocutor ordering the party whose solicitor has withdrawn to appear or be represented at a diet to be held not less than fourteen days (or such other period as the sheriff may order) from the date of the interlocutor. The interlocutor contains a warning that if the party fails to appear or be represented by the diet, the sheriff may grant decree or make such order as he thinks fit.

A copy of the interlocutor and a notice in Form G10 are served on the party whose solicitor has withdrawn, either by the party making the motion referred to above or by any other party appointed by the sheriff. Service is made using one of the methods available for the citation of a defender (see Chapter 7), and a certificate of service must be lodged in process.

Consequences of failure to intimate intention to proceed (r 24.3)

If the party fails to appear or be represented and state his intention to proceed or otherwise, the sheriff may grant decree or make such other order or finding as he thinks fit.

Chapter 27

Minutes of sist and transference

Minutes of sist (r 25.1)

Where any party in the action (pursuer, defender or third party) dies or comes under legal incapacity, e.g. he has become bankrupt, any person claiming to represent such party, such as an executor or trustee in bankruptcy, may apply by minute to be sisted as a party to the cause.

The minute should be set out in standard form but should also seek leave for a date for an Options Hearing to be fixed (see page 45). The normal procedures for intimation, opposition and hearing of minutes apply (see page 45).

Minutes of transference (r 25.2)

Minutes of sist are appropriate where a person other than a party wishes to enter the action. A minute of transference is appropriate where a party in the action wishes to have the cause transferred in favour of or against a representative of a party who has died or come under legal incapacity.

Application is made by minute and the procedure is identical with that for a minute of sist, as described above, except that, in addition to the minute and intimation of minute forms, a copy of the pleadings (including any adjustments or amendments) is served.

Chapter 28

Transfer and remit of causes

Transfer to another sheriff court (r 26.1)

The sheriff has wide powers to transfer an ordinary cause from his own sheriff court to another. There are three ways in which transfer is effected:

(i) where there are two or more defenders and the action has been raised in the sheriff court district in which one defender resides or carries on business, the cause may be transferred to another sheriff court having jurisdiction over one of the defenders;

(ii) where a plea of no jurisdiction has been sustained and the cause is remitted to the sheriff court before which it appears that it ought to have been raised;

(iii) where, on cause shewn, the sheriff decides to remit the cause to another sheriff court, irrespective of jurisdiction.

In cases (i) and (ii), the sheriff may only transfer the cause on the motion of one or more of the parties, but he has an overriding power to transfer if he is satisfied that there is sufficient cause. Transfer of causes is mostly made under head (iii) above, either because parties and/or witnesses reside in a sheriff court district other than that in which the action has been raised or because a connected action is pending before the other sheriff court.

On making the transfer the sheriff must state his reasons in the interlocutor and may make such order on expenses as he thinks fit.

The receiving court must accept the transfer and the cause proceeds as if it has been raised in that court.

The interlocutor is appealable to the Sheriff Principal, with leave of the sheriff, but not beyond.

Remit to the Court of Session (r 26.2)

The sheriff court has privative (exclusive) jurisdiction to deal with all causes not exceeding £1,500 in value exclusive of interest and expenses (s 7, 1907 Act). However, in actions which are not subject to privative jurisdiction, the sheriff may, on the motion of any of the parties to the cause, if he is of the opinion that the importance or difficulty of the cause make it appropriate to do so, remit the cause to the Court of

Session. In any action for divorce or in an action in relation to the custody or adoption of a child, the sheriff may, of his own accord, remit the action to the Court of Session (Sheriff Courts (Scotland) Act 1971, s 37). If, in any proceedings against the Crown, a certificate by the Lord Advocate is produced to the effect that the proceedings may involve an important question of law, or may be decisive of other cases, or are for other reasons more fit for trial in the Court of Session, the sheriff must remit the proceedings to the Court of Session (Crown Proceedings Act 1947, s 44).

Within four days after the sheriff had pronounced an interlocutor remitting the cause to the Court of Session, the sheriff clerk must transmit the process to the deputy principal clerk of session, having, within the same period, sent written notice of the remit to the parties and certified on the interlocutor sheets that he has done so.

Remit from the Court of Session (r 26.3)

The Court of Session may, in relation to an action before it which could competently have been brought before a sheriff, remit the action (at its own instance or on the application of any of the parties to the action) to the sheriff within whose jurisdiction the action could have been brought if, in the opinion of the court, the nature of the action makes it appropriate to do so (Law Reform (Miscellaneous Provisions) (Scotland) Act 1985, s 14).

When the process is received the sheriff clerk must note the date of receipt, enrol the cause on the first court day occurring not earlier than fourteen days after the date of receipt, and send notice of the date of calling to parties.

Chapter 29

Caution and security

Introduction

The finding of caution or giving of security is appropriate in actions in which one party is of the opinion that another party will be unable to meet financial liabilities in the action, e.g. payment of principal sum sued for or expenses. The procedure is particularly appropriate where a pursuer's estate has been sequestrated, in which case the defender may ask the court to sist the trustee in the sequestration as a party to the action failing which the pursuer should be asked to find caution for expenses.

Form of application (r 27.2)

Application for an order for caution or security, or for variation or recall of such an order, is made by written motion, on Form G6, and the usual procedures relating to intimation, opposition and hearings apply (see page 48).

Orders (r 27.3)

The interlocutor containing the order to find caution or give security specifies the period within which caution is to be found or security given.

Before granting an order against a limited company, the sheriff must be satisfied, by credible testimony, that there is reason to believe that the company will be unable to pay the defender's expenses if successful in his defence, and if so satisfied and an order made, proceedings are sisted until caution is found.

Methods of finding caution or giving security (r 27.4)

There are several ways of finding caution or giving security:

(i) by bond of caution;

(ii) by consignation of money into court; or

(iii) by a method other than (i) or (ii), approved by the sheriff, or a combination of (i) and (ii).

Any document by which the order is satisfied must be lodged in process, except where the security, as approved, is in the form of a deposit receipt in joint names of the agents of parties in which case a copy of the deposit receipt, and not the principal, is lodged in process. Any document lodged in satisfaction of the order cannot be borrowed.

Cautioners and guarantors (r 27.5)

Caution is often found by way of a bond supplied by an insurance company, on payment of a premium, but the insurance company must be authorised by the Secretary of State to carry on business on bonds of caution.

Form of bonds and other securities (r 27.6)

Bonds issued by company cautioners are in standard form and contain the wording required by this rule, and a bond issued by an insurance company will state that the company has been duly authorised. It is possible to have a bond issued by an individual cautioner, in which case the sheriff clerk will advise on the acceptability of the wording.

Sufficiency of caution or security and objections (r 27.7)

The sheriff clerk must satisfy himself that any document lodged in respect of the order to find caution or give security is in proper form, but any party who is dissatisfied with the sufficiency or form of the caution or other security offered may apply, by written motion, for decree or such other order as may be appropriate (see below).

Insolvency or death of the cautioner or guarantor (r 27.8)

Where an individual cautioner:

   (i)   becomes apparently insolvent;

   (ii) calls a meeting of creditors to consider the state of his affairs; or

   (iii) dies unrepresented;

or, in the case of a company cautioner,

   (i)   a winding up order has been made;

   (ii) a receiver has been appointed; or

   (iii) a voluntary arrangement in insolvency has been approved,

the party entitled to benefit from the caution or guarantee may apply by motion for a new security or further security to be given.

Failure to find caution or give security (r 27.9)

Where a party fails to find caution or give other security as ordered, any other party may apply by motion:

   (i)   where the party in default is a pursuer, for decree of absolvitor; or

(ii) where the party in default is a defender or third party, for decree by default or such other finding or order as the sheriff thinks fit.

These provisions apply equally to circumstances in which caution or other security has been offered but another party is dissatisfied with the sufficiency or form of the caution or other security.

Chapter 30

Recovery of evidence

Introduction

All parties to the cause are expected to lodge documents or other productions which are founded on in the pleadings or which are relevant to the cause, and there are specific time limits within which such documents or other productions must be lodged (see page 62). If any party, having been lawfully required to do so, fails to lodge a document or other production which is in his custody or power, remedies are available to the other parties in the cause. Application may be made for:

(i) a commission and diligence; or

(ii) an order under section 1 of the Administration of Justice (Scotland) Act 1972 (as amended).

Execution of a commission and diligence can be a lengthy and expensive procedure; an optional procedure, which is quicker and less expensive, is available.

Orders under section 1 of the 1972 Act are similar in nature to a commission and diligence so far as documents or other productions are concerned but, additionally, the court has power to order any person to disclose such information as he has as to the identity of any person who might be a witness or defender in the action.

In most cases, evidence in the proof in an action is given by witnesses attending the court but there are circumstances in which this may not be practicable, e.g. a witness may be too ill to attend the court or may reside outwith the jurisdiction of the court. Special arrangements can be made to deal with this type of situation.

(i) The court may appoint a commissioner to take the evidence of a witness who cannot attend court.

(ii) A letter of request may be addressed to a court or tribunal outside Scotland to take the evidence of a witness located in the jurisdiction of such court or tribunal.

(iii) Evidence which is in danger of being lost, e.g. because the witness is seriously ill or has to go abroad, may be taken by the sheriff or a commissioner before the diet or proof, to lie *in retentis* until the case goes to proof.

Applications for commission and diligence for recovery of documents or for orders under section 1 of the Act of 1972 (r 28.2)

Application for:

(i) a commission and diligence for recovery of documents; or

(ii) an order under section 1 of the 1972 Act,

is made by motion in Form G6 and should be accompanied by a specification of:

(i) the document or other property sought to be inspected, photographed, preserved, taken into custody, detained, produced, recovered, sampled or experimented on or with, as the case may be; or

(ii) the matter in respect of which information is sought as to the identity of a person who might be a witness or a defender,

which is lodged in process.

A copy of the motion and specification is served in the usual way on:

(i) every other party;

(ii) any third party who has the document, other property or information sought; and

(iii) where public records or public servants are involved, the Lord Advocate, who may appear at the hearing of the motion.

If the sheriff grants a motion for the recovery etc of documents or other property etc, a commissioner is appointed by the sheriff to execute the commission and report back to the court.

If a motion on information as to the identity of a person is granted, a certified copy of the interlocutor granting the motion is served on the person who is the subject of the order.

Optional procedure before executing commission and diligence (r 28.3)

It is open to the party who has obtained a commission and diligence for the recovery of a document to instruct the commissioner to proceed but, before doing so, he may elect to use the following optional procedure:

(i) an order, with certificate attached, in terms of Form G11 is prepared;

(ii) the order and a specification of the document(s) to be produced are served, by registered or first class recorded delivery post, and may be posted to the solicitor acting for the party or haver from whom the documents are to be recovered;

(iii) the person to whom the order is addressed is directed to lodge with the sheriff clerk all documents in the specification which are in his possession, by hand or by registered or first class recorded delivery post, within seven days from service of the order;

(iv) in addition to any documents in the specification, there must be lodged with the sheriff clerk:

- an inventory of the documents lodged;
- the original order; and
- a signed and completed certificate (see (vi) below);

(v) if the possessor of the documents claims confidentiality, the documents must be lodged but may be placed in a sealed packet marked 'confidential' — see also page 76;

(vi) the certificate, in Form G11, should reflect whichever of the following circumstances applies:

- that the documents produced are all of the documents in the possession of the recipient of the order which are in the specification; or
- that the recipient has no documents in his possession which are in the specification; or
- that documents in the specification exist, but were last seen in the hands of a (named) person on a specific date; or
- that the recipient knows of no other person in possession of any documents in the specification.

When the order, certificate and inventoried documents (if any) have been received by the sheriff clerk, he sends notice to the solicitors of all parties to the cause that the order has been obtempered. The notice specifies which, if any, of the documents in the specification have been lodged.

The party who served the order has an exclusive right to borrow any of the documents for a period of seven days from the date of the official intimation. Thereafter the other parties to the cause may borrow the document.

If the party serving the order fails to uplift the document within seven days, the sheriff clerk intimates such failure to every other party — and where no party has uplifted the document within fourteen days after such intimation, the sheriff clerk returns the document to the haver who delivered it to him. Where a party has uplifted the document but does not wish to lodge it in process, he must return it to the sheriff clerk who intimates the return to all other parties and, if no other party uplifts the document within fourteen days after such intimation, the sheriff clerk returns the document to the haver.

The purpose of the optional procedure is to reduce expense. However, if the party who served the order is dissatisfied with the results, for example if he is of the view that full production has not been made or that adequate reason for non-production has not been given, he may revert to commission and diligence procedure.

If extracts from books are produced, the sheriff, on cause shown, may order that the party obtaining the commission be allowed to inspect the originals and take copies but if confidentiality is claimed, the sheriff may direct that inspection and copy-taking be carried out in the presence of the appointed commissioner. The sheriff may order the production of any books (except bankers' books or books of public record) notwithstanding the production of certified extracts.

If the person to whom the notice is addressed fails to obtemper it, the party who served the order may report the fact to the sheriff who will make such order, if any, which he thinks fit, or the party who served the order may instruct the commissioner to execute the commission.

Execution of commission and diligence for recovery of documents (r 28.4)

The sheriff may preside over the execution of diligence, but it is usual for the sheriff to appoint a commissioner to act on his behalf.

The party seeking to execute the commission must:

(i) provide the commissioner with:
- a copy of the specification of documents;
- an up-to-date copy of the pleadings; and
- a certified copy of his appointment;

(ii) instruct the clerk and any shorthand writer considered necessary by the commissioner or any party; and

(iii) be responsible for the fees of the commissioner and his clerk, and of any shorthand writer.

The commissioner, in consultation with the parties in the action, fixes a diet for the execution of the commission, and the party seeking to execute the commission arranges service of a citation in Form G13 on the haver with a copy of the specification and, where considered necessary, an up-to-date copy of the pleadings.

Parties and the haver may be represented by a solicitor, or person having a right of audience before the sheriff, at the execution of the commission.

If a shorthand writer is present at the commission, he is sworn in by the commissioner. A haver takes the oath in Form G14 or, where he elects to affirm, in Form G15.

Following the hearing, the commissioner sends:

(i) a report of the execution of diligence;

(ii) any document recovered; and

(iii) an inventory of such documents,

to the sheriff clerk.

The sheriff clerk intimates the receipt of the report, document and inventory (if any) to all parties, and thereafter the procedure for uplifting the document etc is identical to that under the optional procedure (see page 73).

Execution of orders for production or recovery of documents or other property under section 1(1) of the Act of 1972 (r 28.5)

An order made on an application under section 1(1), for production or recovery of documents or other property, includes the grant of a commission and diligence, and the optional procedure and procedure for the execution of a commission, as explained above, apply equally to the execution of an order.

Execution of orders for inspection etc of documents or other property under section 1(1) of the Act of 1972 (r 28.6)

An order made on an application under section 1(1) for inspection etc of documents or other property in the hands of a haver is executed by a person specified in the interlocutor. A copy of the interlocutor, specification and, where necessary, an up-to-date set of pleadings, is served on the haver.

Execution of orders for preservation of documents or other property under section 1(1) of the Act of 1972 (r 28.7)

An order for preservation, custody and detention of a document or other property includes the grant of a commission and diligence for detention and custody of such document or other property.

The party obtaining the order:

(i)   provides the commissioner with:
- a copy of the specification;
- a copy of up-to-date pleadings; and
- a certified copy interlocutor of his appointment;

(ii) is responsible for payment of the fees of the commissioner and his clerk; and

(iii) serves a copy of the order on the haver.

The execution of the commission and diligence follows the usual procedure (see page 75), after which the commissioner sends:

(i)   a report of the execution;

(ii) any document or other property taken by the commissioner; and

(iii) an inventory of such property,

to the sheriff clerk to await the further orders of the sheriff.

Confidentiality (r 28.8)

If any party to the cause or a haver, having been required to produce a document or other property, under:

(i)   a commission and diligence;

(ii) the optional procedure; or

(iii) an order under the Act of 1972,

claims confidentiality for the document or other property produced, the document must be enclosed in a sealed packet and marked 'confidential'. The packet cannot be opened, or put in process, unless the sheriff on the motion of:

(i)   the party who obtained the commission and diligence; or

(ii) any other party, after the date of intimation by the sheriff clerk of failure to uplift documents (see above),

grants leave.

Normal procedures for dealing with motions apply and, in addition, a copy of the motion is served, by first class recorded delivery service, on the haver. The person claiming confidentiality may oppose the motion.

Warrants for production of original documents from public records (r 28.9)

Extracts from public records are normally acceptable as productions in an ordinary cause. If it is necessary to produce the original register or deed from either the Keeper of the Registers of Scotland or the Keeper of the Records of Scotland, the following procedure must be followed:

(i)   the party wishing to obtain the register or deed should write to the Keeper in charge of the originals giving notice of his intention to request production;

(ii) not earlier than seven days after giving notice, a written motion should be lodged, specifying the registers or deeds to be produced;

(iii) if the sheriff is satisfied that it is necessary for the ends of justice that the motion should be granted, he signs an interlocutor, including specification of the registers and deeds and the date of the proof or hearing, to that effect;

(iv) the party should write to the Deputy Principal Clerk of Session, enclosing a copy of the sheriff's interlocutor, duly certified by the sheriff clerk or one of the deputes, for an order from the Lords of Council and Session authorising the Keeper to exhibit the original register or deed to the sheriff;

(v)   the Deputy Principal Clerk submits the application to a Lord Ordinary in Chambers and, if warrant is granted, a certified copy of the warrant is served on the Keeper;

(vi) the production is not given to the party. A member of the Keeper's staff will bring it to the proof or hearing for inspection and will thereafter return it to the Keeper; and

(vii) any expense incurred in the transmission or exhibition of the production falls to be defrayed in the first instance by the party making the application.

Commissions for examination of witnesses (r 28.10)

The court may appoint a commissioner:

(i) to take the evidence of a witness who:

- resides beyond the jurisdiction of the court; or
- resides within the jurisdiction but at some place remote from the court; or
- by reason of age, infirmity or sickness, is unable to attend the diet of proof (so far as age is concerned, normal practice is that a witness over the age of 70 should not be compelled to attend court but may have his evidence taken on commission); or

(ii) to take the evidence of a witness which is in danger of being lost, to lie *in retentis*.

Application for the appointment of a commissioner is made by motion specifying the name and address of at least one commissioner for approval and appointment by the sheriff. The normal procedure on motions applies. If the motion is granted, the commissioner is in much the same position as the sheriff, and the interlocutor granting the commission is authority for citing witnesses to appear at the hearing.

At the commission, the commissioner swears in the shorthand writer (if any), and witnesses attending to give evidence either take the oath in Form G14 or, where a witness elects to affirm, the affirmation in Form G15.

The commission follows the same procedure as a proof before the sheriff, without interrogatories (see below), unless, on cause shown, the sheriff otherwise directs.

Commissions on interrogatories (r 28.11)

Interrogatories are a list of questions to be put to a witness, such as:

1. Do you know the defender?
2. How long have you known him?
3. In what circumstances did you first meet him?

Interrogatories are appropriate where parties' solicitors are not present when the witness attends before the commissioner.

The party who has obtained a commission for the examination of witnesses, and in circumstances which warrant interrogatories, must lodge draft interrogatories in process and any other party may lodge cross-interrogatories. Both documents are then subject to adjustment and agreement between parties, and are extended and lodged with the sheriff clerk for approval. Any areas of dispute are settled by the sheriff.

The party who has obtained the commission must:

(i) provide the commissioner with:

- an up-to-date copy of the pleadings;

- the approved interrogatories and any cross-interrogatories; and
- a certified copy of the interlocutor containing his appointment;

(ii) instruct the clerk; and

(iii) be responsible, in the first instance, for the fee of the commissioner and his clerk.

The commissioner, in consultation with parties, fixes a diet for the execution of the commission, and the party who has obtained the commission cites the witness using Form G13, suitably adapted.

After the execution of the commission, the commissioner sends to the sheriff clerk:

(i) the executed interrogatories;

(ii) any document produced by the witness; and

(iii) an inventory of any such document.

Not later than the day after he receives the above, the sheriff clerk intimates to each party that he has received them.

The party who obtained the commission must lodge in process:

(i) the report of the commission; and

(ii) the executed interrogatories and any cross-interrogatories.

Commissions without interrogatories (r 28.12)

Where interrogatories are not involved, i.e. the witness will be examined and cross-examined by parties' solicitors, the party who has obtained the commission must:

(i) provide the commissioner with:
  - an up-to-date copy of the pleadings; and
  - a certified copy of the interlocutor of his appointment;

(ii) fix a diet for the execution of the commission in consultation with the commissioner and every other party;

(iii) instruct the clerk and any shorthand writer;

(iv) be responsible for the fees of the commissioner, the clerk and any shorthand writer; and

(v) cite the witness using Form G13 suitably adapted.

The execution of the commission is conducted in the same way as a proof, and parties are entitled to be present or represented. Any questions of relevancy or admissibility of evidence led at the execution are reserved for the sheriff.

After the execution of the commission, the commissioner sends:

(i) a report of the execution of commission;

(ii) any document produced by the witness; and

(iii) an inventory of any such documents,

to the sheriff clerk who, not later than the day after receipt, intimates to each party that he has received them.

The party who obtained the commission must lodge the commissioner's report in process.

Evidence taken on commission (r 28.13)

The evidence taken on commission may be used as evidence at the proof, by any party to the cause, subject to any objection to its use, relevancy or admissibility — any such objections are determined by the sheriff. If the witness becomes available to give evidence at the proof, the evidence taken before the commissioner will not be used.

Letters of request (r 28.14)

Where a witness is resident outwith Scotland, or documents or other property are located outwith Scotland, application may be made for letters of request addressed to the court or tribunal within whose jurisdiction the witness resides or the documents etc are located.

The application is made by minute in Form G16, and a proposed letter of request in Form G17. If the application relates to the evidence of a witness, interrogatories and cross-interrogatories must be drawn up and agreed (see page 78). The normal procedure for dealing with minutes applies.

If the application is granted, the solicitor for the applicant is personally liable for all expenses connected with the letter of request and with any witness who may be examined, and must consign into court such sum as the sheriff thinks fit to meet such expenses.

The applicant must lodge a translation of the letter of request, interrogatories and cross-interrogatories into the official language of the country in which the court or tribunal is situated, unless English is the official language or the sheriff clerk certifies that no translation is required.

The letter of request, any interrogatories and cross-interrogatories and translations (if any) are sent by the sheriff clerk to the Foreign and Commonwealth Office or to such other person and in such manner as the sheriff may direct. The completed interrogatories, and any productions, documents or other property are returned through the Foreign and Commonwealth Office to the sheriff clerk.

Citation of witnesses and havers (r 28.15)

The citation of witnesses and havers to a commission follows the standard procedure for the citation of witnesses (see page 83) except that the period of notice is fixed by the commissioner and, although the rules do not require the party citing the witness to lodge a certificate of citation, it would be prudent to lodge such a certificate as a precaution in the event of the witness refusing or failing to appear. A warrant for second diligence may be issued to compel a witness to attend (see page 84), and if a witness fails to answer a citation the sheriff may grant warrant for the apprehension of the witness (see page 85).

Chapter 31

Proof

Reference to oath (r 29.1)

Reference to oath is rare, if not unknown, in practice. Its main use is in cases in which it is the only means of proof, for example to establish a loan in the absence of writing. The oath of the deponent takes the place of a proof.

Application for a reference is made after the record has been closed and preliminary pleas disposed of, and takes the form of a minute lodged with the sheriff clerk. The minute may be signed by the party making the reference or by his solicitor, in which case the solicitor should have written authority to apply for the reference. The sheriff may grant the reference (and attach whatever conditions he thinks fit) or refuse it.

If the party to whose oath reference has been made fails to appear at the diet, the sheriff may hold him as confessed and grant decree.

Remit to person of skill (r 29.2)

When an action is concerned with technical matters, such as building construction, accounting or repairs to machinery, it may be preferable to have a person who is well acquainted with the technicalities to examine the matter and report back to the court. The procedure is known as a remit to a person of skill and is designed to render unnecessary proof of the matter dealt with by the reporter. Lists of persons qualified and willing to act as reporters are maintained by most professional and trade associations.

Application for a remit may be made by any party or on a joint motion. Where application is made by one of the parties, a motion should be lodged and the normal procedure for intimation, opposition etc applies, and the expenses of the remit will, in the first instance, be met by that party. If the remit is made by joint motion, the report is final and conclusive with respect to the subject matter of the remit, and the expenses of the remit will, in the first instance, be met by parties equally, unless the sheriff otherwise directs.

Evidence generally (r 29.3)

Affidavit evidence has been limited to certain family actions hitherto, but is now extended to all ordinary actions.

Any party may apply by motion for:

(i) the evidence of a witness to be received by affidavit; and/or

(ii) a specified statement or document to be admitted as evidence without calling as a witness the maker of the statement or document,

and the sheriff, after considering the affidavit, statement or document as the case may be, may make such order as he thinks fit.

Renouncing probation (r 29.4)

Following the closing of the record, it is normal to fix a proof or, if there are preliminary pleas, a debate. However, if the parties are agreed that the action does not raise questions of fact but only law, they may forgo the right to a proof and lodge a joint minute to that effect with the sheriff clerk, with or without a statement of admitted facts and productions, and the sheriff, if satisfied that it is right to do so, will order the case to be debated.

Orders for proof (r 29.5)

At the Options Hearing, if the sheriff decides that a proof is necessary, he fixes a diet for taking proof.

The most common mode is proof at large. The sheriff allows the parties a proof of their respective averments, parole (oral) evidence is led by the examination of witnesses, the solicitors acting for parties address the sheriff on the evidence, and a judgment is issued by the sheriff.

While most proofs consist of parole evidence, it may be that part of a case can only be proved by writ, in which case the sheriff may fix a proof *habili modo*. This leaves it to the discretion of the sheriff to decide on the type of evidence to be led.

The sheriff may limit the mode of proof, e.g. by excluding proof of averments which are irrelevant, by restricting proof of specified averments to the writ or oath of the defender. The limitation should be contained in the interlocutor ordering the proof.

Hearing parts of proof separately (r 29.6)

If the action has pecuniary conclusions, the sheriff may, on his own motion or on the motion of any party, order that proof on liability or any specified issue be heard separately from proof on the question of the amount for which decree may be pronounced, and he may decide the order in which the separate proofs will be heard.

Citation of witnesses (r 29.7)

Witness citations are normally sent by post (registered post or first class recorded delivery service) by the solicitor acting for the party on whose behalf the witness is cited. If this method fails, a sheriff officer may be instructed to effect service (and, in the case of a party litigant, the initial service is by the sheriff officer — see below). If the method used by the sheriff officer involves depositing or affixing the citation at the person's dwelling place or place of business, a letter containing a copy of the citation must be sent by ordinary post to the address at which he thinks it most likely that the person may be found.

The fact that a proof has been allowed and a diet fixed is normally sufficient authority for the citation of witnesses. If, for any reason, the authority to cite is challenged or if it is anticipated that it will be challenged, a copy of the interlocutor allowing the proof, certified by the sheriff clerk, should be obtained.

Witnesses must be cited on seven days' notice, in Form G13, and the party citing the witness must lodge a certificate of citation in Form G12.

The solicitor who cites the witness is personally liable for his fees and expenses, and if a solicitor, having cited a witness, intimates to the witness that the citation has been cancelled, he must advise the witness that the cancellation does not affect any other citation that the witness may have received from another party in the cause.

Citation of witnesses by party litigants (r 29.8)

The only way in which a party litigant may cite witnesses is by instructing a sheriff officer, and, by the same token that a solicitor is personally liable for fees and expenses of a witness cited by him, the party litigant has to satisfy the court that witnesses' fees and expenses will be met by the party litigant.

The party litigant must prepare and lodge a motion showing:

(i) the number of witnesses he proposes to cite; and

(ii) the period for which they may be required to attend court,

not later than four weeks before the diet of proof, requesting the sheriff to fix caution in such sum as the sheriff considers reasonable, having regard to the amount of expense likely to be incurred. If the motion is granted, before instructing a sheriff officer to cite a witness, the party litigant must find caution for such expenses as may be expected to be incurred by the witness.

Second diligence against a witness (r 29.9)

If it is anticipated that a witness will fail to attend a diet of court, for example because a postal citation has been returned marked 'Refused', the party citing the witness may produce a valid certificate of citation and apply for letters of second diligence which, if granted, authorise a sheriff officer to arrest the witness. The letters also authorise the sheriff officer to imprison the witness, but the normal procedure is to bring him before the bar of the court when the sheriff may decide to imprison him or order him to attend a further diet of court, with or without finding caution for his appearance.

Decree for the expenses of the application may be granted against the witness.

Failure of witness to attend (r 29.10)

If, at the time of proof or hearing, a witness fails to attend, having been duly cited, the sheriff, on the motion of the party who cited the witness, and on production of a valid certificate of citation, may grant warrant for the apprehension, by a sheriff officer, of the witness and for bringing him to the court.

There is a possibility that, if the witness is apprehended on the day of the proof or hearing, he can be brought before the court on that day and his evidence taken.

A witness must be given at least seven days' notice to attend a diet. He is advised in the citation that he may ask for travelling expenses to be paid to him in advance. If he has been given sufficient notice and travelling expenses, if any were requested, and fails to attend the diet, he will be liable to a penalty, not exceeding £250, unless the sheriff was satisfied that there was reasonable excuse for the failure. Any penalty is payable to the party on whose behalf the witness was cited, and a decree will be granted for its recovery.

Lodging productions (r 29.11)

All documents and other productions must be lodged, with an inventory, on or before the fourteenth day before the date fixed for proof. At the same time, notice of the lodging must be sent to all other parties in the cause.

If any party wishes to lodge any document or other production after the above date, he must have either the consent of the other parties or the permission of the sheriff, who may make an order on expenses or otherwise as seems just.

The productions, having been lodged, may be borrowed but must be returned not later than 12.30 on the afternoon of the day preceding the diet of proof.

Copy productions (r 29.12)

For the convenience of the sheriff before, during and after the proof, a copy of every production, marked with the appropriate number of process, and securely fastened if consisting of more than one sheet, must be lodged for the use of the sheriff, not later than forty-eight hours before the diet of proof.

Returning borrowed parts of process and productions before proof (r 29.13)

All parts of process and productions which have been borrowed must be returned to the sheriff clerk before 12.30 pm on the day preceding the diet of proof.

Notices to admit and notices of non-admission (r 29.14)

If matters relevant to the cause can be identified as non-contentious before the case goes to proof, and if agreement can be reached between parties, the need for the attendance of witnesses to speak to such matters can be avoided and expense saved. It is open to parties to lodge a joint minute of admissions specifying facts, circumstances etc which are not in dispute; but any party can serve a notice on any other party calling on that party to admit:

(i) such facts relating to an issue averred in the pleadings; or

(ii) the authenticity of a document or copy document lodged in process.

Service of the notice is carried out in the same way as intimation of parts of process or adjustments (see page 40).

If the party receiving the notice agrees with the subject matter of the notice, he should advise the party serving the notice within fourteen days of receiving intimation.

If the party receiving the notice:

(i) does not admit a fact specified in the notice; or

(ii) does not admit, or seeks to challenge, the authenticity of a document specified in the notice,

he must, within twenty-one days of receipt of intimation, intimate, by the method referred to above, a notice of non-admission to the party who intimated the notice.

If a party fails to intimate a notice of non-admission:

(i) he is deemed to have admitted the fact or document specified in the notice; and

(ii) if the failure to intimate is not made within fourteen days of the date of intimation, he will be liable for expense incurred in proving the fact or document.

A deemed admission is restricted to the party by whom it is deemed to be made and the cause in which it is deemed to be made.

Copies of all notices must be lodged in process.

Instruction of shorthand writer (r 29.15)

Where a shorthand writer is to record evidence at a proof, the responsibility for instructing the shorthand writer lies with the pursuer.

Administration of oath or affirmation to witnesses (r 29.16)

Witnesses are sworn in by the sheriff in Form G14 or, where the witness elects to affirm, in Form G15.

Proof to be taken continuously (r 29.17)

Proof should be taken continuously, i.e. day by day, but the sheriff may adjourn the diet from time to time, for example because a witness is unavailable.

Recording of evidence (r 29.18)

Traditionally, evidence in a proof is recorded by a shorthand writer and for the foreseeable future this will continue to be the case, but the rules provide for the introduction of tape-recording of evidence in civil courts in the same way as is the method used in criminal courts.

Evidence is recorded, by shorthand writer or tape-recorder, unless parties, by agreement and with the approval of the sheriff, dispense with the recording of evidence.

The cost of the shorthand writer or tape-recording is borne, in the first instance, by parties in equal proportions (this may change eventually when liability for expenses is decided), and solicitors for parties are personally liable for fees payable subject, if necessary, to the sheriff making an order directing payment to be made.

In addition to the evidence of witnesses, the record must include:

(i)   any objection taken to a question or line of evidence;

(ii) any submission made in relation to such an objection; and

(iii) the ruling of the court thereon.

The transcript, or extension, of the record of evidence:

(i)   can be made only on the direction of the sheriff, and the cost in the first instance is borne:

- in an undefended case, by the solicitor for the pursuer; and
- in a defended case, by the solicitors for the parties in equal proportions;

(ii) provided for the use of the court (the sheriff's copy), must be certified as a faithful record by:

- the shorthand writer; or
- the person who transcribed the record from a tape-recording;

(iii) may be altered by the sheriff as appears to him to be necessary, after hearing the parties — any such alterations must be authenticated by the sheriff;

(iv) may be copied to any party on payment of the transcriber's fee;

(v)   except with leave of the sheriff, may be borrowed only for the purpose of enabling a party to consider whether or not to appeal against the interlocutor of the sheriff on the proof.

Where no transcript of the record of evidence has been made, but a transcript is required for appeal purposes, the appellant may request a copy from the shorthand writer or otherwise, on payment of the cost by the solicitor for the appellant in the first instance. The transcript is lodged in process and copies may be obtained by any party on payment of the appropriate fee.

If the services of a shorthand writer or tape-recording have been dispensed with, the sheriff, if called on to do so, must:

(i) record in a separate note the terms of objections to the admissibility of evidence on the grounds of confidentiality or to the production of a document on any ground, and his decision thereon; and

(ii) in all other cases, record in the note to his interlocutor disposing of the merits of the cause, the terms of objections and his decision.

The provisions for recording evidence described above apply equally to the recording of evidence at a commission.

Incidental appeal against rulings on confidentiality of evidence and production of documents (r 29.19)

A party to the cause or other person (e.g. a witness or haver), who objects to the admissibility of oral or documentary evidence on the ground of confidentiality, or to producing a document on any ground, and is dissatisfied with the ruling of the sheriff may, with leave of the sheriff, appeal to the Sheriff Principal who must dispose of the appeal with the least possible delay. No other form of appeal against a decision of the sheriff on admissibility of evidence or production of documents is competent during the proof.

The sheriff may proceed with the parts of the proof which are not dependent on the ruling appealed against.

An appeal against the decision of a commissioner requires leave of the sheriff.

Parties to be heard at close of proof (r 29.20)

The hearing on evidence may proceed immediately after the close of proof whether or not the evidence has been recorded by a shorthand writer. In complicated cases it might be considered desirable to have the shorthand notes extended, in which case the hearing takes place at a later date.

Having heard parties or their procurators on the evidence, the sheriff may pronounce judgment there and then or he may make avizandum (reserve judgment).

Chapter 32

Decrees, extracts and execution

Introduction

Decree, which includes any judgment, deliverance, interlocutor, act, order, finding or authority which may be extracted, may be pronounced on the merits of the case or for expenses. The need to apply for an extract of the decree arises when it is likely that diligence will have to be executed to enforce the decree. The issue of an extract of a decree has important effects on time limits for appeal and, as a general rule, application for an extract decree is made as a matter of course.

Taxes on money under the control of the court (r 30.2)

All monies paid into court, e.g. as a means of finding caution (see page 69), are entered in a register of consignations kept by the sheriff clerk in terms of the Sheriff Court Consignations (Scotland) Act 1893. No decree, warrant or order for payment of the consigned money to any person may be granted until there has been lodged with the sheriff clerk a certificate by an officer of the Inland Revenue that all taxes or duties payable to the Inland Revenue have been paid or satisfied.

Decree for payment in foreign currency (r 30.3)

Where decree has been granted for payment of a sum of money in a foreign currency, or the sterling equivalent, the party requesting an extract must, by minute endorsed on or annexed to the writ, state the rate of exchange prevailing:

(i) on the date of decree; or

(ii) on the date, or within three days before the date, on which the extract is ordered,

and the sterling equivalent at that rate for the principal sum and interest decerned for, together with a certificate in Form G18.

When decrees are extractable (r 30.4)

A decree in absence may be extracted after the expiry of fourteen days from the date of decree, and is usually ordered when the initial writ is lodged with a crave for decree and expenses.

An extract of a decree in a defended cause may be issued after the expiry of fourteen days from the date of decree unless:

(i)   an appeal has been marked (in which case, an extract may be issued on the date on which the appeal has been finally disposed of); or

(ii) an application for leave to appeal has been lodged; or

(iii) the sheriff has allowed extract to be applied for and issued earlier; or

(iv) the sheriff has reserved the question of expenses (in which case, an extract may be issued only after the expiry of fourteen days from the date of the interlocutor dealing with expenses, unless the sheriff otherwise directs).

In the case of (iii) above, the motion for early issue of an extract must either be made in the presence of parties, or the sheriff must be satisfied that written intimation of the motion has been given to all other parties.

Apart from the above provisions, the sheriff has power to supersede extract until a date later than fourteen days from the date of decree.

Extract of certain awards notwithstanding appeal (r 30.5)

The only circumstances in which the marking of an appeal does not prevent the issue of an extract decree are in family actions in which an award of custody, access or aliment has been made, unless an order has been made excusing obedience to or implement of the award.

Form of extract decree (r 30.6)

The forms are in Appendix 2.

Form of warrant for execution (r 30.7)

The extract contains the words:

'This extract is warrant for all lawful execution hereon',

which authorise a sheriff officer to execute whatever diligence is necessary to implement the decree.

Date of decree in extract (r 30.8)

Where the Sheriff Principal has adhered to the decision of the sheriff following appeal, the date to be inserted in the extract decree as the date of decree is the date of the decision of the Sheriff Principal.

Service of charge where address of defender is not known (r 30.9)

As a general rule, the defender in an action must be given written notice (a charge) by a sheriff officer that a decree has been granted or an order has been made against him and that a period of time must expire before the decree or order can be enforced. In ordinary causes the period of time (or days of charge) is fourteen days.

If the address of the defender is unknown, the charge will be deemed to have been served on the defender if it is:

(i) served, by the sheriff officer, on the sheriff clerk of the district where the defender's last known address is located; and

(ii) displayed by the sheriff clerk on the walls of court (notice board) for the period of the charge, which starts on the day the charge is displayed.

On the expiry of the period of charge, the sheriff clerk endorses a certificate on the charge that it has been properly displayed, and returns the charge to the sheriff officer.

Chapter 33

Appeals

The following modes of appeal are available in ordinary causes:

(i) from the sheriff to the Sheriff Principal;

(ii) from the sheriff to the Court of Session; and

(iii) from the Sheriff Principal to the Court of Session.

The mode will depend on the types of interlocutor against which the appeal is taken, and leave to appeal may be required.

Appeal to the Sheriff Principal

The following interlocutors may be appealed from the sheriff to the Sheriff Principal without leave:

(i) a final judgment, i.e. an interlocutor which, by itself, or taken along with other interlocutors, disposes of the subject matter of the cause, notwithstanding that judgment may not have been pronounced on every question raised, and that expenses found due may not have been modified, taxed or decerned for;

(ii) an interlocutor granting or refusing interdict — interim or final;

(iii) an interlocutor granting an interim decree for payment, other than expenses;

(iv) an interlocutor making an order *ad factum praestandum;*

(v) an interlocutor sisting an action;

(vi) an interlocutor allowing, refusing, or limiting the mode of proof;

(vii) an interlocutor refusing a reponing note.

An appeal may be marked against any interlocutor which the sheriff, either *ex proprio motu* or on the motion of any party, grants leave to appeal (1907 Act, s 27).

Appeal to the Court of Session

The following interlocutor may be appealed from the Sheriff Principal or the sheriff to the Court of Session without leave:

(i) a final judgment (as defined above);

(ii) an interlocutor granting an interim decree for payment of money other than a decree for expenses;

(iii) an interlocutor sisting an action;

(iv) an interlocutor refusing a reponing note.

An appeal may be marked against any interlocutor against which the Sheriff Principal or sheriff, either *ex proprio motu* or on the motion of any party, grants leave to appeal (1907 Act, s 28).

Time limit for appeal (r 31.1)

Any interlocutor which does not require leave to appeal against it, may be appealed within fourteen days of the date of the interlocutor, unless it has been extracted following a motion for early extract (see page 90).

Application for leave to appeal (r 31.2)

Interlocutors referred to above (see paragraphs headed *Appeal to the Sheriff Principal* and *Appeal to the Court of Session*) may be appealed without leave being granted. All other interlocutors may be appealed only with leave of the sheriff or Sheriff Principal as the case may be. Application for leave to appeal must be made within seven days of the date of the interlocutor against which it is desired to appeal, and if the application is for leave to appeal from a decision in relation to a time to pay direction or the recall or restriction of an arrestment, the application must specify the question of law on which the appeal is made. Application is not competent if the interlocutor has been extracted following a motion for early extract. If leave is granted, the appeal must be marked within seven days of the granting of leave.

Form of appeal and notice to parties (r 31.3)

The appeal takes the form of a written note on:

(i) the interlocutor sheet; or

(ii) any other written record containing the interlocutor; or

(iii) a separate sheet lodged with the sheriff clerk.

It should be in the following terms:

'The [pursuer, applicant, claimant, defender, respondent or other party] appeals to [the Sheriff Principal or The Court of Session]'

and should be signed by the appellant and show the date on which it is signed.

If the appeal is to the Sheriff Principal, the sheriff should be requested to append a note to his interlocutor, if he has not done so, by adding the words 'and requests the sheriff to write a note' (see page 42).

If the appeal is to the Court of Session the note of appeal must specify the name and address of the solicitor or other agent who will be acting for the appellant.

Within four days of the appeal being marked the sheriff clerk must:

(i) send written notice of the appeal to all other parties to the cause and certify on the interlocutor sheet that he has done so; and

(ii) transmit the process to the Sheriff Principal or the Court of Session (Deputy Principal Clerk of Session) as the case may be.

Failure by the sheriff clerk to send notice or certify as above will not invalidate the appeal.

Reclaiming petition or oral hearing (r 31.4)

An oral hearing is the most common procedure for an appeal before the Sheriff Principal. He may order a reclaiming petition and answers in which the arguments for parties are set out, but this method is almost unknown in practice. If all parties are agreed that neither a reclaiming petition nor an oral hearing is necessary, they may move the Sheriff Principal to dispose of the appeal accordingly.

Appeals in connection with custody, access or aliment (r 31.5)

Where an appeal is marked against an interlocutor containing an award of custody, access or aliment, the marking of the appeal does not excuse obedience to or implement of the award unless by order of the sheriff, the Sheriff Principal or the Court of Session.

Interim possession etc pending appeal (r 31.6)

The judge against whose judgment an appeal is taken (Sheriff Principal or sheriff), may make orders relating to:

(i) interim possession;

(ii) the preservation of any property to which the action relates, or for its sale, if perishable;

(iii) the preservation of evidence; or

(iv) any matter which the judge considers necessary in the interests of parties.

These orders, once made, are not subject to reviews except by the Appellate Court (the Court of Session or Sheriff Principal).

Abandonment of appeal (r 31.7)

An appeal to the Sheriff Principal having been marked, it can be abandoned only with the consent of all parties or by leave of the Sheriff Principal. There is no procedure in the sheriff court for abandonment of an appeal marked to the Court of Session.

Chapter 34

Taxation of expenses

Taxation before decree for expenses (r 32.1)

If expenses are moved for in an undefended cause, it is normal practice to elect to charge an inclusive fee as fixed in the table of fees. This is an optional procedure — the pursuer may alternatively move for expenses as taxed by the auditor of court. This latter is the normal procedure in decrees *in foro*, in which case the sheriff allows an account of expenses to be given in and remits the account, when lodged, to the auditor of court to tax the account and report back to the court.

Decree for expenses in name of solicitor (r 32.2)

When the account of expenses has been taxed, the sheriff is asked to grant decree for the taxed amount. At this stage, the solicitor acting for the party moving for decree may ask the sheriff to allow the decree for expenses to be extracted in his name, the effect being that the solicitor can recover the expenses for himself separately from any other recovery action by the client against the debtor.

Procedure for taxation (r 32.3)

Where the sheriff has allowed an account of expenses to be remitted to the auditor of court for taxation:

(i)   the account is lodged with the sheriff clerk;

(ii) the account and process are transmitted by the sheriff clerk to the auditor of court;

(iii) on receipt of the account, the auditor assigns a diet for the taxation not earlier than seven days from the date he receives the account;

(iv) the auditor intimates the diet forthwith to the party who lodged the account;

(v)   the party who lodged the account must forthwith send a copy of the account to all other parties and advise them of the date, time and place fixed for the taxation;

(vi) any or all parties may decide not to attend the taxation;

(vii) if parties are present, they may make representation on the amount of any item in the account;

(viii) the auditor may conclude the taxation at the diet or adjourn the diet for further consideration, in which case, he must inform parties who attended the taxation of his decision;

(ix) when the account has been taxed, the auditor returns the process and account to the sheriff clerk; and

(x) if no note of objection is lodged, the sheriff may grant decree for the expenses as taxed.

Objections to auditor's report (r 32.4)

A note of objections to the taxed account may be lodged, but only by a party who attended the taxation; the note must be lodged within seven days of the diet of taxation, or, where the auditor reserved consideration of the account (see (viii) above), within seven days of the date on which the auditor intimated his decision.

The sheriff must dispose of the objections in a summary manner, with or without answers.

Chapter 35

Family actions

Part I — General provisions

Introduction

The term 'family action', as defined in the Rules, includes:

(i) an action of divorce;

(ii) an action of separation;

(iii) actions of declarator of:

- legitimacy;
- illegitimacy;
- parentage;
- non-parentage; and
- legitimation;

(iv) an action or application for any parental rights;

(v) an action of affiliation and aliment;

(vi) an action of, or application for or in respect of, aliment;

(vii) an action or application for financial provision after a divorce or annulment in an overseas country;

(viii) an action or application for an order under the Matrimonial Homes (Family Protection) (Scotland) Act 1981; and

(ix) an application for the variation or recall of an order made by the Court of Session in respect of maintenance, custody etc.

Averments in actions of divorce or separation about other proceedings (r 33.2)

In actions of divorce or of separation it is obligatory to insert an article of condescendence specifying whether any proceedings are continuing (i.e., not finally disposed of) in Scotland or elsewhere in respect of the marriage to which the initial writ relates. If there are proceedings which are continuing, the articles of condescendence must specify:

(i) the court, tribunal or authority before which they have been commenced;

97

(ii) the date of commencement;

(iii) the names of the parties;

(iv) whether a proof or hearing has been appointed and, if so, the date; and

(v) any other facts which might assist the sheriff to determine whether the action before him should be sisted in terms of Sch 3 to the Domicile and Matrimonial Proceedings Act 1973.

(Information about continuing proceedings, as mentioned above, must also be inserted in any defences or minutes lodged by any party if it is additional to or contradictory of the information provided by the pursuer, or if the pursuer has provided no such information.)

Averments where custody sought (r 33.3)

This rule applies to an application for a custody order in an action which has other craves, e.g. for divorce or separation. Independent applications for custody orders are covered by ss 10 and 12 of the Family Law Act 1986.

Application for a custody order (which includes access) in an action of divorce or separation must include an averment giving particulars of any other proceedings known to the applicant, whether in Scotland or elsewhere, and whether concluded or not, which relate to the child in respect of whom the order is sought, and, in any other family action, in addition to the above averment, the applicant must include averments giving particulars of any proceedings known to him which are continuing, whether in Scotland or elsewhere, and which relate to the marriage of the parents of the child.

(Information about continuing proceedings, mentioned above, must be inserted in any defences or minute lodged by any party, if it is additional to or contradictory of the information provided by the applicant or if the applicant has provided no such information.)

Averments where the identity or address of a person is not known (r 33.4)

The nature and circumstances of any family action determine the type of intimation to be given to interested parties, and the types of information are set out in detail in r 33.7 (see below).

Where the identity or address of any person to whom intimation is requested is unknown and cannot reasonably be ascertained, the party required to apply for the warrant (normally the pursuer) must aver that fact and set out what steps have been taken to ascertain the identity or address as the case may be.

Averments about maintenance orders (r 33.5)

Where in a family action an order for aliment or periodical allowance is sought, or is sought to be varied or recalled, by any party, the pleadings of that party must contain an averment stating whether and, if so, when and by whom, a maintenance order has been granted in favour of or against that party or of any other person in respect of whom the order is sought.

Averments where aliment or financial provision is sought (r 33.6)

(a) Introduction

The purpose of this rule is to ensure that there is no overlap in the roles of the sheriff and the Child Support Agency in relation to aliment or child support maintenance.

(b) Top up orders

Even though the Agency has fixed the amount of child support maintenance payable, the sheriff has power to make an order for additional payments (top up maintenance orders), and where a family action contains a crave for aliment or for recall or variation of a decree for aliment and the provisions relating to top up maintenance orders apply, the initial writ must include averments stating, where appropriate:

   (i)   that a maintenance assessment (by the Agency) is in force;

   (ii) the date of the maintenance assessment;

   (iii) the amount and frequency of payments under the assessment; and

   (iv) the grounds on which the sheriff retains jurisdiction, and

should be accompanied by any document issued by the Agency to the party intimating the making of the maintenance assessment.

(c) Provisions of the Child Support Act do not apply

Where in a family action a crave for aliment, or for variation or recall of a decree for aliment, is included, and the action is presented on the basis that the provisions in the Child Support Act relating to top up maintenance do not apply, the initial writ must include averments stating:

   (i)   that the habitual residence of the absent parent, person with care or qualifying child (all within the meaning of the Act), is furth of the United Kingdom;

   (ii) that the child is not a child within the meaning of the Act; or

   (iii) where the action is lodged for warranting before 7 April 1997, the grounds on which the sheriff retains jurisdiction.

(d) Non-parentage or illegitimacy

In an action for non-parentage or illegitimacy, the pursuer must include an article of condescendence stating whether he previously has been alleged to be the parent in an application for a maintenance assessment carried out by the Agency; where an allegation of paternity has been made against the pursuer, the Secretary of State must be named as a defender in the action.

(e) Decisions by Child Support Agency

Where, in any family action involving parties, a decision has been made by the Agency in any application, review or appeal under the Act relating to any child of the parties, the initial writ or defences must include averments that such a decision has been made and give details of the decision and, unless the sheriff otherwise directs, be accompanied by any document issued by the Agency intimating that decision.

Warrants and forms for intimation (r 33.7)

(a) Introduction

The first procedural step in the majority of ordinary actions is the grant of a warrant to cite the defender. Under the previous Rules, in cases in which there was a requirement for intimation on a person other than the defender, this was dealt with as a separate procedural step but, under the new Rules, where there is such a requirement, the pursuer must include a crave for a warrant of intimation in the initial writ. Consideration must be given to whether or not such a crave needs to be included in the initial writ and, if so, it should read: 'to grant warrant for intimation on EF, within designed'.

Where the identity or address of any person in respect of whom a warrant of intimation is required to be applied for is not known and cannot reasonably be ascertained, the initial writ must contain averments setting out what steps have been taken to ascertain the identity or address (see r 33.4), and, in certain actions (which are identified below), where the address of a person to whom intimation is required is not known and cannot reasonably be ascertained, the pursuer must include a crave to dispense with intimation, and the sheriff may grant the crave or make such other order as he thinks fit.

(b) Craves for warrant for intimation in family actions

(i) Address of defender not known

Where the address of the defender is not known and cannot reasonably be ascertained, the pursuer must include a crave for a warrant for intimation to:

(a) every child of the marriage between the parties who has reached the age of 16; and

(b) one of the next-of-kin of the defender who has reached that age, unless the address of such person cannot reasonably be ascertained. Where the address is known, a notice in Form F1 and a copy of the initial writ must be intimated to such person.

(ii) Allegation of adultery

Where the pursuer alleges that the defender has committed adultery with another person, and:

(a) such person is named in the initial writ, a copy of the initial writ and notice of intimation in Form F2 must be intimated to such person; or

(b) such person is named in the initial writ and there is an averment that his or her address is not known and cannot reasonably be ascertained, the pursuer must include a crave in the initial writ to dispense with intimation.

There is no need to crave a warrant for intimation if:

(a) the person is not named in the initial writ, but there should be an averment setting out what steps have been taken to ascertain the identity of such person; or

(b) the pursuer alleges that the defender has been guilty of rape upon or incest with such person.

(iii) Defender suffering from mental disorder

Where the defender is suffering from a mental disorder, the pursuer must include a crave for a warrant for intimation on:

(a) every child of the marriage between the parties who has reached the age of 16; and

(b) one of the next-of-kin of the defender who has reached that age; and

(c) the *curator bonis* to the defender, if one has been appointed,

in Form F3 attached to a copy of the initial writ. (See also r 33.13.)

(iv) Polygamous marriage

Where an action relates to a marriage entered into under a law which permits polygamy, and:

(a) the pursuer seeks a decree of:

• divorce;

• nullity of marriage;

• separation;

• aliment;

• declarator that the marriage is valid or invalid; or

• any other decree involving a determination as to the validity of the marriage; and

(b) either party to the marriage in question has any spouse additional to the other party,

a copy of the initial writ and notice of information in Form F4 must be intimated to such additional spouse unless the address of such person is not known and cannot reasonably be ascertained, in which case the initial writ must contain a crave to dispense with intimation.

(v) Parental rights

Where, in an action for divorce or separation, the sheriff may make an order for parental rights in respect of a child:

(a) who is:

- in the care of a local authority; or
- liable to be maintained by a third party,

a copy of the initial writ and a notice of intimation in Form F5 must be intimated to such local authority or third party as the case may be; or

(b) in respect of whom a third party exercises such rights *de facto*, a copy of the initial writ and a notice of intimation in Form F6 must be intimated to such third party.

If the address of a third party, as referred to above, is not known and cannot reasonably be ascertained, the pursuer must include a crave in the initial writ to dispense with intimation.

(vi) Custody — application by parent

Where the pursuer craves the custody of his child, and the other parent or the guardian of the child is not a party to the action, a copy of the initial writ and notice of intimation in Form F7 must be intimated to such parent or guardian unless the address of such parent or guardian is not known and cannot reasonably be ascertained, in which case the pursuer must include a crave in the initial writ to dispense with intimation.

(vii) Custody — application by non-parent

Where the pursuer craves the custody of a child, and he is:

(a) not a parent of that child; and

(b) resident in Scotland when the initial writ is lodged,

a copy of the initial writ and a notice of intimation in Form F8 must be intimated to the local authority within whose area the pursuer resides. (See also r 33.12.)

(viii) Custody — pursuer not resident in Scotland

Where the pursuer craves the custody of a child, and is not resident in Scotland when the initial writ is lodged for warranting, he must include a crave for an order for intimation in Form F8 to such local authority as the sheriff thinks fit. (See also r 33.12.)

(ix) Action which affects a child

In any family action which affects a child who is not a party to the action, a copy of the initial writ and notice of intimation in Form F9 must be intimated to that child unless the address of that child is not known and cannot reasonably be ascertained, in which case the pursuer must include a crave in the initial writ to dispense with intimation.

The terms of the rule notwithstanding, there may be reasons why it would be undesirable to send notice of the action to a child, e.g. because of the child's age, in which case it might be preferable to include a crave to dispense with intimation and to include averments in support of such a crave in the condescendence.

(x) Transfer of property

In an action for divorce, either party to the marriage may apply for an order for the transfer of property to him by the other party; if the pursuer makes such an application, and:

(a) the consent of a third party to such a transfer is necessary; or

(b) the property is subject to a security,

a copy of the initial writ and a notice of intimation in Form F10 must be intimated to such third party or creditor, as the case may be, unless the address of such third party or creditor is not known, in which case the pursuer must include a crave in the initial writ to dispense with intimation.

(xi) Avoidance transaction

If one party in an action for aliment or a claim for financial provision claims that the transfer or transaction involving property carried out by the other party had the effect, or is likely to have the effect, of defeating the action or claim referred to above, he or she may apply for an order to prevent or set aside the transfer or transaction; in any action in which such an application is made, a copy of the initial writ and notice of intimation in Form F11 must be intimated to:

(a) any third party in whose favour the transfer or transaction is to be or was made; and

(b) any other person having an interest in the transaction,

unless the address of such third party or other person is not known and cannot reasonably be ascertained, in which case the pursuer must include a crave in the initial writ to dispense with intimation.

(xii) Matrimonial homes

In an action where the pursuer makes an application for an order under the Matrimonial Homes (Family Protection) (Scotland) Act 1981, and:

(a) he is a non-entitled partner, and the entitled partner has a spouse, a copy of the initial writ and notice of intimation in Form F12 must be intimated to that spouse; or

(b) the application relates to occupancy rights, exclusion orders etc (specified in the rule), and the entitled spouse or entitled partner is a tenant or occupies the matrimonial home by permission of a third party, a copy of the initial writ and notice of intimation in Form F12 must be intimated to the landlord or the third party, as the case may be.

(c) Notices of intimation under r 33.7

Notices of intimation under this rule are on a period of notice of twenty-one days unless the sheriff otherwise orders, but no period of notice must be less than two days. Each form of notice includes guidance or instruction on action to be taken (if any).

(d) Where identity or address becomes known

If, during the course of the action, the identity or address of any person to whom intimation is required becomes known, the party who would have been required to include a crave for warrant of intimation must lodge a motion for a warrant of intimation to that person or to dispense with such intimation.

Intimation where improper association is alleged (r 33.8)

Where, in a family action, the pursuer alleges sodomy, incest or a homosexual relationship between the defender and a named person who is not a party to the action, no intimation is ordered until the period of notice has expired, when the pursuer must lodge a motion for an order for intimation or to dispense with intimation. The sheriff may order intimation or dispense with it. In the latter case, he may also order that the name of the third party be deleted from the condescendence of the initial writ. If intimation is ordered, a copy of the initial writ and an intimation in Form F13 is intimated to the named person.

Productions in action of divorce or where order for custody may be made (r 33.9)

In an action:

(i) of divorce, the marriage certificate, or equivalent document, must be lodged with the initial writ;
(ii) in which the sheriff may make a custody order, the birth certificate of each child, or an equivalent document, must be lodged.

Otherwise a warrant to cite will not be granted by the sheriff clerk, unless the sheriff otherwise directs.

Warrant of citation (r 33.10)

The warrant of citation in family actions is in Form F14.

Form of citation and certificate (r 33.11)

(a) Citation and certificate

As a general rule, the citation of a defender in a family action is in Form F15, attached to a copy of the initial writ and warrant of citation (Form

F14), together with a notice of intention to defend in Form F26 and, after service, a certificate of citation in Form F16 is attached to the initial writ.

The exceptions to the general rule are:

(i)   where the address of the defender is not known (see r 5.6);

(ii) where a local authority is named as a defender (see r 33.12);

(iii) where the defender suffers, or appears to suffer, from mental disorder and is in hospital (see r 33.13); and

(iv) in certain actions of divorce or separation based on non-cohabitation (see r 33.14).

(b) Methods of service

The methods of service of family actions are the same as those for ordinary actions in general, namely:

(i)   postal service (see r 5.3);

(ii) service within Scotland by sheriff officer (see r 5.4);

(iii) service on persons furth of Scotland (see r 5.5); and

(iv) service where the address of a person is not known (see r 5.6).

Execution of service on, or intimation to, a local authority (r 33.12)

In actions in which a custody order is sought by:

(a) a non-parent resident in Scotland; or

(b) a pursuer not resident in Scotland,

and a local authority is named as a defender in the initial writ at the time it is lodged, service must be executed within seven days after the date of granting a warrant of citation, and is made by serving a copy of the initial writ, with Form F8 attached, on the local authority; and in cases in which intimation of an application for a custody order is to be made to a local authority, intimation must be made within seven days after the date on which a warrant of citation, or an order for intimation, as the case may be, has been granted.

Service in cases of mental disorder of the defender (r 33.13)

In a family action where the defender suffers or appears to suffer from a mental disorder, and is resident in a hospital or similar institution, a citation in Form F15 is sent, by registered post or first class recorded delivery service, to the medical officer in charge, along with:

(i)   a copy of the initial writ;

(ii) any notice required by r 33.14(1) (see next page);

(iii) a request, in Form F17, that the medical officer deliver and explain the initial writ, citation and any notice or form of notice of consent personally to the defender;

(iv) a certificate in Form F18 for the medical officer to complete by certifying either that delivery and explanation have been made, or that they have not been made because to do so would be dangerous to the health or mental condition of the defender; and

(v) a stamped envelope addressed for return of the medical officer's certificate to the pursuer or his solicitor, if he has one.

When the certificate is returned, it should be attached to the certificate of citation (Form F16).

If the medical officer has decided not to deliver the initial writ etc to the defender, and has completed the certificate to that effect, the sheriff may order further medical enquiry and such service of the initial writ as he thinks fit.

Notices in certain actions of divorce or separation (r 33.14)

In terms of section 1 of the Divorce (Scotland) Act 1976, ordinary actions of divorce or of separation may be raised:

(i) after non-cohabitation between the pursuer and defender for a continuous period of two years where the defender consents to decree; or

(ii) without consent of the defender where the continuous period of non-cohabitation is for a period of five years or more.

The circumstances on which the action is based are narrated in the condescendence in the normal way.

Service of the initial writ includes statutory notices which are designed to inform the defender of such matters as the effect of decree and consent (where appropriate) including withdrawal of consent.

Notice or notices (in terms of Forms in the schedule) to be sent with the service copy initial writ depend on the type of action.

Divorce

(i) two years' non-cohabitation and consent: Forms F19 and F20,

(ii) five years' non-cohabitation: Form F23.

Separation

(i) two years' non-cohabitation and consent: Forms F21 and F22,

(ii) five years' non-cohabitation: Form F24.

The certificate of citation (Form F16) must state which notice or form has been attached to the initial writ (see also r 33.18 below).

Orders for intimation by sheriff (r 33.15)

The sheriff has power, in any family action, to order intimation to be made to such person as he thinks fit; and where any party makes an application or averment which, if made in the initial writ, would have required a warrant for intimation (see r 33.7 above), that party must lodge a motion for a warrant for intimation or to dispense with such intimation.

Appointment of curators *ad litem* to defenders (r 33.16)

The purpose of this rule is to afford protection to a defender, in an action of divorce or of separation, who may be suffering from mental disorder, and also to overcome the possible difficulty of obtaining written consent from the defender in such circumstances.

Where it appears to the sheriff that the defender is suffering from mental disorder, as mentioned above, the sheriff must appoint a curator *ad litem* (a person appointed by the court to look after the defender's interests in the action), and the pursuer must send a certified copy of the initial writ and defences (if any), and a copy of the Options Hearing notice (if any) sent to him by the sheriff clerk, to the curator within seven days of the appointment.

If the action is for divorce on the basis of two years' non-cohabitation and the consent of the defender is required, the sheriff will make an order informing the Mental Welfare Commission for Scotland and requesting it to report on whether the defender is capable of deciding whether or not to give consent to the granting of decree.

Within fourteen days of the Commission submitting a report or, if no report has been called for, within twenty-one days of his appointment, the curator may lodge:

(i) a notice of intention to defend;

(ii) defences;

(iii) a minute adopting defences already lodged; or

(iv) a minute stating that he does not intend to lodge defences.

In any event, the curator may appear in the action at any time to protect the interests of the defender.

If, at any time, it appears to the curator *ad litem* that the defender is not suffering from mental disorder, he may report that fact to the court and seek his discharge.

The pursuer is responsible, in the first instance, for payment of the fees and outlays of the curator *ad litem* incurred during the period of his appointment until:

(i) he lodges a minute stating that he does not intend to lodge defences;

(ii) he decides to instruct the lodging of defences or a minute adopting defences already lodged; or

(iii) being satisfied that the defender is not suffering from mental disorder, he is discharged.

Application for sist (r 33.17)

Schedule 3 to the Domicile and Matrimonial Proceedings Act 1973 provides a procedure whereby an action of divorce or separation may be sisted before the beginning of the proof, if other proceedings in respect of the marriage are continuing in another jurisdiction and certain conditions (specified in the schedule) are met.

Application for a sist of procedure, or recall of a sist of procedure, must be made by written motion.

Notices of consent to divorce or separation (r 33.18)

In actions of divorce or of separation where the defender's consent to decree is necessary (see r 33.14 above), a form of consent is enclosed with the service copy initial writ. If the defender consents to decree, he or she is required to sign Form F20 or F22, as the case may be. The completed form is sent to the sheriff clerk who lodges it in process.

If the defender does not consent to decree, or if he or she wishes to withdraw a consent already given, the defender should give notice in writing to the sheriff clerk, who intimates the terms of the notice to the pursuer.

The next stage in the procedure depends on whether or not the initial writ contains other averments that there has been an irretrievable breakdown in the marriage, for example that the defender has committed adultery; and if so the action will proceed in the normal way.

If there are no such averments, the pursuer must enrol a motion, within fourteen days of receiving intimation from the sheriff clerk, to have the action sisted and the sheriff may grant the motion. If no such motion is lodged, the pursuer will be deemed to have abandoned the action which will be dismissed. If procedure has been sisted, and the sist has been neither recalled nor renewed within a period of six months from the grant of the sist, the pursuer is deemed to have abandoned the action, which will be dismissed.

Consents to grant of custody (r 33.19)

Custody of a child will not be granted in any proceedings to a person other than a parent or guardian of the child unless certain conditions (specified in section 47(2) of the Children Act 1975) are met, including, in some cases, the consent of a parent or guardian of the child.

In cases where such a consent is required, the party requiring it, when executing service on or giving intimation to the person who may give consent, must:

(i) include with a copy of the initial writ or other pleadings, as the case may be:

- a notice in Form F7; and
- a form of notice of consent in Form F25; and

(ii) in the certificate of service or intimation, state that such notice and form were included.

If the parent or guardian consents to the grant of an application for custody, he is required to sign Form F25, have his signature witnessed, and return the form to the sheriff clerk. If the person giving consent wishes to withdraw consent, he must give notice in writing to the sheriff clerk, who intimates the terms of the notice to every other party.

Reports by local authorities under s 49(2) of the Children Act 1975 (r 33.20)

Where an applicant for custody of a child is not a parent of the child, an order awarding custody to that applicant will not, except on cause shown, be made unless the applicant has given due notice to the appropriate local authority in Form F8 (see pages 102 and 105). On receipt of a notice, the local authority must investigate and report to the court on all the circumstances of the child and on the proposed arrangements for the care and upbringing of the child.

On completion of the report, the local authority must:

(i) send the report, with a copy for each party, to the sheriff clerk; and

(ii) where a curator *ad litem* has been appointed to the child, send a copy of the report to him.

The sheriff clerk sends a copy of the report to each party.

In actions where this rule applies, no application for custody can be determined until the report is lodged. When disposing of the application, the sheriff decides which party (or parties) is to be liable for the expenses of the local authority incurred in the preparation of the report.

Appointment of local authority or reporter to report on a child (r 33.21)

At any stage of a family action, the sheriff may call for a report on the circumstances of a child and on any proposed arrangements for the care and upbringing of the child. The sheriff may appoint either the local authority or a person outwith the local authority to investigate and report.

On making the appointment, the sheriff directs who will instruct the local authority or reporter and who will be responsible, in the first instance, for expenses incurred by the local authority or reporter, and the person so directed must, within seven days of the appointment, intimate the name and address of the local authority or reporter, as the case may be, to any local authority to which intimation of the family action has already been made (see page 105).

On completion of the report, the local authority or reporter, as the case may be, must send the report, with a copy for each party, to the sheriff clerk who then sends a copy of the report to each party. In actions where this rule applies, no application for custody can be determined until the report is lodged.

Referral to family mediation and conciliation service (r 33.22)

Where custody of, or access to, a child is in dispute, the sheriff may at any stage refer the dispute to a specified family mediation and conciliation service.

Application for orders to disclose the whereabouts of children (r 33.23)

Where, in proceedings for or relating to a custody order in respect of a child, there is not available to the court adequate information as to where the child is, the court may order any person who it has reason to believe has relevant information to disclose it to the court. An application for such an order must be made by written motion. If the sheriff makes such an order, he may order the person against whom the order has been made to appear before him or lodge an affidavit.

Applications in relation to removal of children (r 33.24)

This rule relates to the threatened or actual removal of a child from the care and possession of a person or from the jurisdiction of the court.

Section 51(1) of the Children Act 1975 provides:

'Where a person has applied for the custody of a child, it shall be an offence, except with the authority of a court ... to remove the child from the care and possession of the applicant against the will of the applicant ...'

Section 35(3) of the Family Law Act 1986 provides:

'A court in Scotland ... may ... grant interdict or interim interdict prohibiting the removal of the child from the United Kingdom ... or out of the control of the person in whose custody the child is.'

Application for authority to remove the child or for interdict or interim interdict prohibiting removal of the child from the jurisdiction is made by motion if the applicant is a party to the action and, if not, by minute.

Service or intimation of an application for interdict could be self-defeating, and an application may be made without service or intimation.

An application under s 23(2) of the Child Abduction and Custody Act 1985 for a declarator that the removal of a child from the United Kingdom was unlawful is a prerequisite for the return of the child under the Convention on the Civil Aspects of International Child Abduction, and must be made:

(i) in a pending action:
- by a party, in the initial writ, defences or minute as the case may be, or by motion; or
- by any other person, by minute; or

(ii) after final decree, by minute in the process.

Intimation to the local authority before supervised access (r 33.25)

Arrangements for access to children, whether by agreement of parties or by order of the court, normally proceed on an unsupervised basis, but the sheriff may, on his own motion or on the motion of a party, make an award of access or interim access subject to supervision by a social worker, but before doing so the sheriff requires to be satisfied that adequate arrangements, involving social work department resources, can be made.

The party moving for supervised access must intimate to the chief executive of the local authority (where it is not already a party to the action and represented at the hearing at which the issue arises):

(i) the terms of the motion;

(ii) the intention of the sheriff to order that access be supervised by the social work department; and

(iii) that the local authority must, within the period fixed by the sheriff:
- notify the sheriff clerk whether it intends making representations to the sheriff; and
- if so, to do so within the period fixed.

Joint minutes (r 33.26)

This rule clarifies the question of whether a joint minute can be given effect to, even though to do so involves granting decree in respect of matters for which there is no crave in the pleadings. The sheriff may interpone the authority of the court to a joint minute relating to:

(i) parental rights of a child;

(ii) aliment for a child; or

(iii) an order for financial provision,

without there being a crave.

Affidavits (r 33.27)

The sheriff may accept evidence by affidavit (in lieu of parole evidence) at any hearing for an order or interim order.

Part II — Undefended family actions

Evidence in certain undefended actions (r 33.28)

Actions of divorce, actions of separation and actions for declarator of parentage, non-parentage, legitimacy, legitimation or illegitimacy can be classified as undefended:

(i) where no notice of intention to defend has been lodged; or

(ii) where the court has directed the action to proceed as undefended, including an action being defended otherwise than on the merits.

Before granting decree in such actions, the sheriff has to be satisfied that the averments in the initial writ have been proved, and, unless the sheriff otherwise directs, proof is by evidence given on affidavit.

Separate provisions apply to actions mentioned above in which a curator *ad litem* has been appointed (see page 107). Affidavit evidence is admissible in such actions only if the curator *ad litem* to the defender has lodged a minute intimating that he does not intend to lodge defences.

Separate provisions apply also to the following family actions, if proceeding as undefended:

(i)   for parental rights (see below);

(ii) for aliment (see page 120);

(iii) of affiliation and aliment (see page 27);

(iv) for financial provisions after an overseas divorce or annulment (see page 120); and

(v)   for an order under the Matrimonial Homes (Family Protection) (Scotland) Act 1981 (see page 123).

'Affidavit' includes an affirmation and a statutory or other declaration, and must be sworn or affirmed before:

(i)   a notary public;

(ii) a justice of the peace;

(iii) a commissioner of oaths; or

(iv) a statutory authority within the meaning of the Statutory Declarations Act 1835.

A written statement by a qualified medical practitioner, and signed by him, is admissible in place of parole evidence.

Unless the sheriff otherwise directs, evidence relating to the welfare of a child must be given by affidavit, at least one affidavit being emitted by a person other than a parent or party to the action.

Practice Notes issued by Sheriff's Principal give detailed guidance on the preparation and content of affidavits.

Procedure for decree in actions under r 33.28 (r 33.29)

In undefended family actions in which affidavit evidence is appropriate (as described above), affidavits may be lodged after the expiry of the period for lodging a notice of intention to defend, and should be accompanied by the initial writ with a minute in Form F27 endorsed thereon.

The sheriff considers the whole cause and, without requiring the pursuer to attend, may grant decree or other order in terms of the minute or may remit the cause for such other procedure, including proof by parole evidence, as he thinks fit.

Extracts of undefended decree (r 33.30)

In undefended family actions in which affidavit evidence is appropriate and decree has been granted, an extract of the decree is sent to the pursuer and defender by the sheriff clerk after the expiry of fourteen days after the grant of decree. The issue of extracts is automatic; no request is necessary.

Procedure in undefended actions for parental rights (r 33.31)

In an undefended action for any parental rights or authority relating to the welfare or upbringing of a child, it is not necessary to prepare and lodge affidavits, and the normal procedure for decree in absence applies. After the expiry of the period for lodging a notice of intention to defend, the initial writ, with a minute craving decree with expenses, is lodged.

The cause is dealt with by the sheriff in chambers (under the previous rules this type of case had to be called in open court) and decree may be pronounced after such enquiry as the sheriff thinks fit. The sheriff must be satisfied as to the proposed arrangements for the care and upbringing of the child, and, if necessary, he will postpone his decision and call for a report on such arrangements, in terms of the Matrimonial Proceedings (Children) Act 1958, s 11.

No recording of evidence (r 33.32)

Evidence in a proof in an ordinary action is normally recorded by a shorthand writer or by mechanical means, but no record of evidence is necessary in a proof in a family action which is undefended.

Disapplication of Chapter 15 (r 33.33)

Chapter 15 of the Rules sets out the procedure for lodging of, intimation of, opposition to and hearing of motions. It does not apply to family actions in which no notice of intention to defend has been lodged. This permits the sheriff to deal with motions in such actions in the manner he considers to be appropriate.

Part III — Defended family actions

Notice of intention to defend and defences (r 33.34)

If the defender in a family action seeks:

  (i) to oppose any crave in the initial writ;

 (ii) to make a claim for:

    (a) aliment (see page 94);

    (b) an order for:

- the payment of a capital sum (see page 118);
- the transfer of property (see page 118);
- the making of a periodical allowance (see page 118); or
- an incidental order; or

    (c) an order relating to parental rights (see pages 115 and 122); or

(iii) an order:

    (a) setting aside or varying agreements as to financial provisions (see page 118);

    (b) relating to avoidance transactions (see page 119);

    (c) under the Matrimonial Homes (Family Protection) (Scotland) Act 1981 (see page 123); or

(iv) to challenge the jursidiction of the court,

he must:

  (i) lodge a notice of intention to defend in Form F26; and

 (ii) make any claim or seek any order, as the case may be, mentioned above, in the defences by setting out in the defences:

- craves;
- averments in support of such craves; and
- appropriate pleas-in-law.

Abandonment by pursuer (r 33.35)

A pursuer may abandon a cause at any time before decree of absolvitor or dismissal (see page 64) but, if he does so in a family action, the court may allow a defender to pursue an order or claim sought in his defences — and the proceedings in relation to that order or claim then continue as a separate cause.

Attendance of parties at Options Hearing (r 33.36)

The standard procedure in defended causes described in Chapter 12 applies equally to defended family actions, the only difference being that, in a defended family action, all parties must, except on cause shewn, attend personally the Options Hearing.

Decree by default (r 33.37)

The procedure involved in a decree by default in a defended family action is similar to that for other defended actions (see page 50). There are two main differences.

Firstly, where a party fails to lodge a production or part of process or fails to intimate or implement an order (omissions which would normally place the party in default), the sheriff may, on cause shewn, prorogate the time within which lodging, intimation or implement, as the case may be, has to be completed.

Secondly, where there is default in an action of:

(i) divorce;

(ii) separation;

(iii) declarator of legitimacy;

(iv) declarator of illegitimacy;

(v) declarator of parentage;

(vi) declarator of non-parentage;

(vii) declarator of legitimation;

(viii) or application for parental rights,

the sheriff may allow the action to proceed as undefended (see page 112).

Part IV — Applications and orders relating to children in certain actions

Applications in actions to which this Part applies (r 33.39)

This Part applies to an action of divorce or separation (for parental rights in actions other than of divorce or separation, see Part IX). Application in such an action for:

(i) any parental rights; and/or

(ii) aliment for a child,

must be made:

(i) by a crave in the initial writ or defences; or

(ii) where the application is made by a person other than the pursuer or defender, by minute in the action.

Intimation before committal to care or supervision (r 33.40)

Where, in an action of divorce or separation, it appears to the sheriff that there are exceptional circumstances making it impracticable or undesirable for the custody of a child to be entrusted to either of the parties to the marriage, the sheriff may, if he thinks fit, make an order committing the care of the child to any other individual or a local authority; or if satisfied that it is desirable that the child should be under the supervision of an independent person, the sheriff may, as respects any period during which the child is committed to the custody of any person, make an order placing the child under the supervision of a local authority.

Where the sheriff is considering making either a committal to care order or a supervision order, as described above, he will ordain one of the parties to intimate to the individual or local authority, as the case may be, where such individual or local authority is not already a party to the action and represented at the hearing at which the issue arises:

(i)   a copy of up-to-date pleadings;

(ii) the terms of any relevant motion; and

(iii) a notice of intimation in Form F28.

Care or supervision orders (r 33.41)

Where the sheriff makes, varies or recalls a care order or supervision order (as described above), the sheriff clerk must send a copy of the interlocutor making the order and a notice of intimation in Form F29 to the chief executive of the local authority or other person concerned.

Intimation of certain applications to local authorities or other persons (r 33.42)

Where a care or supervision order (as described above) has been made, any motion or minute lodged which relates to the child must be intimated to the chief executive of the local authority or to the other person concerned.

Applications in depending actions by motion (r 33.43)

An application by a party in an action of divorce or separation depending before the court:

(i)   for, or for variation of, an order:
  • for interim aliment for a child under eighteen years; or
  • for interim custody of, or interim access to, a child; or

(ii) for variation or recall of a care or supervision order (as described above),

must be made by motion.

Applications after decree relating to parental rights, care or supervision (r 33.44)

An application after final decree in an action of divorce or separation:

(i) for, or for variation or recall of, an order relating to parental rights; or

(ii) for a care or supervision order (as described above),

must be made by minute in the process of the action to which the application relates and, where such a minute has been lodged, any party to the action may lodge a motion for any interim order which may be made pending determination of the application.

Applications after decree relating to aliment (r 33.45)

An application after final decree in an action of divorce or separation for, or for the variation or recall of, an order for aliment for a child must be made by minute in the process of the action to which the application relates and, where a minute has been lodged, any party may lodge a motion for any interim order which may be made pending determination of the application.

Application after decree by persons over eighteen years for aliment (r 33.46)

An obligation of aliment is owed *inter alia* by:

(i) a father or mother to his or her child; or

(ii) a person to a child who has been accepted by him as a child of his family.

Section 1 of the Family Law (Scotland) Act 1985 defines a 'child' as a person:

(i) under the age of eighteen years; or

(ii) over that age and under the age of twenty-five years who is reasonably and appropriately at an educational establishment, or training for employment or for a trade, profession or vocation.

In an action of divorce or separation, a person:

(i) to whom an obligation of aliment is owed (as described above);

(ii) in whose favour an order for aliment while under the age of eighteen years was made; and

(iii) who seeks, after attaining that age, an order for aliment against the person in that action against whom the order for aliment in his favour was made,

must apply by minute in the process of that action, and an application for interim aliment must be made by motion. Where decree has been pronounced in either of these applications, any application for variation or recall of any such decree must be made by minute in the process of the action to which the application relates.

Part V — Orders relating to financial provision

Introduction

The procedures relating to orders in this Part are limited to actions of divorce, and therefore apply only to the parties to the marriage. Procedures relating to aliment for children are dealt with in Part VIII.

Most of the orders are made under the provisions of the Family Law (Scotland) Act 1985 — referred to in this Part as the Act of 1985.

Applications in actions to which this Part applies (r 33.48)

An application, in an action of divorce, for:

(i) an order for financial provisions within the meaning of s 8(3) of the Act of 1985, i.e.:

- for payment of a capital sum;
- for the transfer of property;
- for the making of a periodical allowance; or
- for an incidental order within the meaning of s 14(2) of the Act of 1985;

(ii) an order setting aside or varying an agreement as to financial provisions;

(iii) an order relating to avoidance transactions; or

(iv) an order for transfer of the tenancy of a matrimonial home,

must be made:

(i) by a crave in the initial writ or defences, as the case may be; or

(ii) where the application is made by a person other than the pursuer or defender, by minute in the action.

Applications in depending actions relating to incidental orders (r 33.49)

Section 14 of the Act of 1985 provides a wide range of incidental orders some of which may be applied for only after decree of divorce has been granted. Rules 33.34 and 33.48 specify, *inter alia*, that applications for incidental orders must be included in the crave of the initial writ or defences but, notwithstanding these rules, in an action depending before the sheriff, application for an incidental order (where competent before decree is granted) may be made by motion and, if the sheriff thinks fit, he will deal with the motion; or he may direct that application should be made in the crave of the initial writ or defences.

An application, in a depending action, for the variation or recall of an incidental order must be made by minute in the process of the action to which the application relates.

Applications relating to interim aliment (r 33.50)

A claim for interim aliment may be made in an action of divorce; an application for, or for the variation or recall of, interim aliment for the pursuer or defender must be made by motion.

Applications relating to orders for financial provision (r 33.51)

After final decree of divorce, an application for:

(i)   a periodical allowance;

(ii) payment of a capital sum or transfer of property;

(iii) variation of date or method of payment of a capital sum or date of transfer of property; or

(iv) variation, recall, backdating or conversion of periodical allowance;

or, after the grant or refusal of decree, an application for:

(i)   an incidental order; or

(ii) variation or recall of an incidental order,

must be made by minute in the process of the action to which the application relates and, where such a minute is lodged, any party may lodge a motion for any interim order which may be made pending the determination of the application.

Applications after decree relating to agreements and avoidance transactions (r 33.52)

An application for an order setting aside or varying agreements as to financial provisions made after final decree must be made by minute in the process of the action to which the application relates. (For applications relating to avoidance transactions, see r 33.53.)

Part VI — Applications relating to avoidance transactions

Form of applications (r 33.53)

An application for an order related to avoidance transactions, by a party in a depending action, must be made by including in the initial writ, defences or minute, as the case may be, appropriate craves, averments and pleas-in-law. An application for such an order after final decree must be made by minute in the process to which the application relates.

Part VII — Financial provision after overseas divorce or annulment

Applications for financial provisions (r 33.55)

Where parties to a marriage have been divorced or the marriage annulled in an overseas country (a country or territory outside the British Islands), then, subject to the jurisdictional requirements and conditions set out in s 28 of the Matrimonial and Family Proceedings Act 1984, an application may be made to the sheriff by one of the parties for an order for financial provision, and such an application is made by initial writ.

Application, made before final decree, for:

(i) transfer of tenancy of the matrimonial home;
(ii) interim periodical allowance; or
(iii) variation or recall of an incidental order,

is made by motion.

Application, made after final decree, for:

(i) variation of:
   • date or method of payment of a capital sum; or
   • date of transfer of property;
(ii) variation, recall, backdating or conversion of a periodical allowance; or
(iii) variation or recall of an incidental order,

is made by minute and, where such a minute has been lodged, any party may apply by motion for an interim order pending determination of the application.

Part VIII — Actions of aliment

Introduction

A claim for aliment only (whether or not expenses are also sought) may be made against any person owing an obligation of aliment in the sheriff court. A claim for aliment may be made in actions of divorce, separations etc but, for the purposes of this Part, unless stated otherwise, it means a claim for aliment only.

Undefended actions of aliment (r 33.57)

Where the pursuer moves for decree in absence in an undefended action of aliment, he must lodge all documentary evidence of the means of the parties available to him in support of the amount of aliment sought.

The sheriff, before granting decree, may require the appearance of parties, in which case the sheriff clerk fixes a hearing.

Applications relating to aliment (r 33.58)

An application for, or for variation of, an order for interim aliment in a depending action of aliment must be made by motion.

After decree has been granted in an action of aliment, an application for the variation or recall of an order for aliment must be made by minute in the process of the action to which it relates, and an application for interim aliment pending determination of such application for variation or recall must be made by motion.

A person to whom an obligation is owed under s 1 of the Family Law (Scotland) Act 1985, in relation to this rule,

(i) by a father or mother to his or her child; or

(ii) by a person to a child who has been accepted by him as a child of his family,

in whose favour an order for aliment while under the age of eighteen years was made in an action of aliment who seeks, after attaining that age, a further order for aliment, must apply by minute in the process of the action to which the application relates, and, pending determination of such application, an application for interim aliment may be made by motion.

Applications relating to agreements on aliment (r 33.59)

In a family action in which a crave for aliment may be made, e.g. in an action of divorce or separation, an application for variation or termination of an agreement on aliment must be made by a crave in the initial writ or defences, as the case may be.

(If no family action has been raised, application for variation or termination must be made by summary application.)

Part IX — Actions relating to parental rights

Introduction

'Parental rights' are defined, in s 8 of the Law Reform (Parent and Child) (Scotland) Act 1986, as:

'tutory, curatory, custody or access ... and any right or authority relating to the welfare or upbringing of a child conferred on a parent by any rule of law'.

This Part applies to an application for parental rights in a family action other than in an action of divorce or separation (for which see page 115).

Form of application (r 33.61)

An application for an order for parental rights must be made:

(i) by an action for parental rights;

(ii) by a crave in the initial writ or defences in a family action other than an action of divorce or separation; or

(iii) where made in one or other of the above actions by a person other than a party to the action, by minute in the action.

Defences in actions for parental rights (r 33.62)

In an action for parental rights, the pursuer must call as a defender:

(i) the parents or other parent of the child in respect of whom the order is sought;

(ii) any guardian of the child;

(iii) any person who has accepted the child into his family;

(iv) any person having the *de facto* custody of the child;

(v) any local authority in whose care or under whose supervision the child is; and

(vi) failing all of the above, the Lord Advocate.

Applications relating to interim orders in depending actions (r 33.63)

An application in a depending action for, or for the variation or recall of, an order for interim custody or interim access must be made:

(i) by a party to the action, by motion; or

(ii) by a person who is not a party to the action, by minute.

Care and supervision by local authorities (r 33.64)

This rule applies to actions other than of divorce or separation. For provisions for actions of divorce or separation, see Part IV.

Where, in an application for the custody of a child, it appears to the sheriff that there are exceptional circumstances making it impracticable or undesirable for the child to be entrusted to either of the parents or to any other individual, the sheriff may commit the care of the child to a local authority; or if either parent or any other person is given the custody of the child but it appears to the sheriff that there are exceptional circumstances making it desirable, he may order that the child should be under the supervision of a local authority.

Where the sheriff is considering making a committal to care order or supervision order, he will ordain one of the parties to intimate to the chief executive of the local authority where such local authority is not already a party to the action and represented at the hearing at which the issue arises:

(i)   a copy of up-to-date pleadings;

(ii) the terms of any relevant motion; and

(iii) a notice of intimation in Form F28.

Where the sheriff makes, varies or recalls a supervision order, the sheriff clerk must send a copy of the interlocutor making the order and a notice of intimation in Form F29 to the chief executive of the local authority.

Where a care or supervision order has been made, any motion or minute lodged which relates to the child must be intimated to the chief executive of the local authority concerned.

Application after decree (r 33.65)

An application after final decree:

(i)   for variation or recall of an order for parental rights; or

(ii) for, or for variation or recall of, a care or supervision order (as described above),

must be made by minute and, where such a minute has been lodged, any party may apply by motion for an interim order.

Part X — Actions under the Matrimonial Homes (Family Protection)(Scotland) Act 1981

Introduction

All actions and applications under this Act proceed as family actions, or as part of a family action, except an application under s 7(1) (dispensing with the consent of a non-entitled spouse to a dealing) or s 11 of the Act (application in relation to poinding) both of which, unless made in a depending family action, are made by summary application.

Forms of application (r 33.67)

Application for an order under the Act is made:

(i)   by an action for such an order;

(ii) by a crave in the initial writ or defences, as the case may be, in any other family action; or

(iii) where the application is made by a person other than a party to the action, by minute.

Defences (r 33.68)

The applicant for an order under the Act must call as a defender:

(i)   where he is seeking an order as a spouse, the other spouse;

(ii) where he is a third party making an application under s 7(1) of the Act (dispensing with the consent of a non-entitled spouse to a dealing) or s 8(1) of the Act (payment from a non-entitled spouse in respect of a loan), both spouses; and

(iii) where the application is made under s 18 of the Act (occupancy rights of cohabiting couples) or that section applies, the other partner.

Applications by motion (r 33.69)

An application for any of the following orders must be made by motion in the process of the depending action to which the application relates:

(i)   interim order for the regulation of the rights of occupancy;

(ii) interim order suspending occupancy rights;

(iii) dispensing with the consent of a non-entitled spouse to a dealing;

(iv) order attaching a power of arrest, if made after an application for matrimonial interdict; and

(v)   extension of the period of occupancy rights.

Intimation of the above motions must be given:

(i)   to the other spouse or partner, as the case may be;

(ii) where the motion is under (i), (ii) or (v) above, and the entitled spouse or partner is a tenant or occupies the matrimonial home by the permission of a third party, to the landlord or third party, as the case may be; and

(iii) to any other person to whom intimation was or is to be made under r 33.7 or r 33.15 (see pages 103 and 107 respectively).

(For the method and form of intimation, see page 48.)

Applications by minute (r 33.70)

An application for:

(i)   variation and recall of orders regulating occupancy and of exclusion order; or

(ii) variation and recall of matrimonial interdict and power of arrest,

must be made by minute.

Intimation of the above minute must be given:

(i)   to the other spouse or partner, as the case may be;

(ii) where the entitled spouse or partner is a tenant or occupies the matrimonial home by the permission of a third party, to the landlord or third party, as the case may be; and

(iii) to any other person to whom intimation was or is to be made under r 33.7 or 33.15 (see pages 103 and 107 respectively).

(For the method and form of intimation, see pages 45 and 46.)

Sist of actions to enforce occupancy rights (r 33.71)

Where an action is or has been raised by a non-entitled spouse to enforce occupancy rights, and application has been made by an entitled spouse or any other person having an interest, for an order dispensing with the consent of a non-entitled spouse to a dealing which has taken place or a proposed dealing, such part of the action which relates to the enforcement of occupancy rights must be sisted until the conclusion of the proceedings on the application, unless the sheriff otherwise directs.

Certificates of delivery of documents to chief constable (r 33.72)

Where the sheriff has granted a matrimonial interdict, which means an interdict, including an interim interdict, which:

(i) restrains or prohibits any conduct of one spouse towards the other spouse or a child of the family; or

(ii) prohibits a spouse from entering or remaining in a matrimonial home or in a specified area in the vicinity of the matrimonial home,

and a power of arrest is attached to the interdict, the applicant spouse must, as soon as possible after service of the interdict on the non-applicant spouse, ensure that there is delivered:

(i) to the chief constable of the police area in which the matrimonial home is situated; and

(ii) if the applicant spouse resides in another police area, to the chief constable of that other police area,

a copy of the application for the interdict and of the interlocutor granting the interdict, together with a certificate of service of the interdict, and where such interdict is varied or recalled, the spouse who applied for the variation or recall must ensure that there is delivered to the chief constable (as described above), a copy of the application for variation or recall and of the interlocutor granting the variation or recall.

The applicant, after complying with either of the delivery requirements described above, must lodge in process a certificate of delivery in Form F30.

Where such a matrimonial interdict ceases to have effect by reason of a decree of divorce being pronounced by the sheriff, the pursuer must send to the chief constable (as described above) a copy of the interlocutor granting decree, and lodge in process a certificate of delivery in Form F30.

Part XI — Simplified divorce applications

Introduction

This is a cheap and simple method of obtaining a decree of divorce in certain uncontested actions. As in all divorce actions, it must be established that there has been an irretrievable breakdown in the marriage, but for the simplified procedure to operate, the reason for the divorce is restricted to the non-cohabitation of the parties over certain periods of time. The written consent of the defender may or may not be necessary, depending on the length of the period of non-cohabitation.

The popular name for the procedure is 'do-it-yourself' because the forms, which are obtainable from the sheriff clerk, are designed for completion by the applicant personally, although they may also be lodged by solicitors.

The grounds of jurisdiction are tiered at national and local levels. An action of divorce is competent under simplified procedure if:

  (i) either party to the marriage is domiciled in Scotland at the date when the action is begun; or

(ii) either party was habitually resident in Scotland throughout the period of one year ending with the date when the action is begun; AND

(iii) either party was resident in the sheriffdom for a period of forty days ending on the date when the action is begun; or

(iv) • the pursuer (applicant) resides furth of Scotland and has been resident in the sheriffdom for a period of not less than forty days ending not more than forty days before the date when the action is begun; or

     • the defender (respondent) has been resident in the sheriffdom for at least forty days ending not more than forty days before the action is begun and has no known residence in Scotland at that date.

Applications under simplified procedure must satisfy the following conditions:

  (i) • two years' non-cohabitation and the defender consents to decree; or

     • five years' non-cohabitation

     (see below for calculation of periods of non-cohabitation);

(ii) no other proceedings are pending in any court which could have the effect of bringing the marriage to an end;

(iii) there are no children of the marriage under sixteen years of age;

(iv) neither party applies for an order for financial provision; and

  (v) neither party suffers from mental disorder.

If an application to the court fails to satisfy all of the above conditions at any time before it is finally disposed of, it must be dismissed.

In calculating the periods of non-cohabitation, no account is taken of any period or periods, not exceeding six months in all, during which the parties cohabit (in an attempt at reconciliation). For example, if during the period of non-cohabitation, there has been cohabitation for a period of five months, application may be made not earlier than two years and five months or five years and five months, as the case may be, from the date of the original separation.

Forms of application (r 33.74)

Forms of application, which are specified in the schedule to the rules, are available on request from the sheriff clerk. The forms are:

- F31: application based on two years' non-cohabitation; and
- F33: application based on five years' non-cohabitation.

A guide to simplified procedure (Form SP1) is issued with each form.

The applicant must complete the following procedure before lodging the application with the sheriff clerk:

(a) Two years' non-cohabitation

Part 1 of the form must be completed and signed by the applicant, after which the form, together with Form F32 (issued with F31), is sent to the respondent by the applicant for completion and signature of part 2 of the form — the consent to divorce. Thereafter the form is returned to the applicant. If the respondent does not complete and sign the consent, the application cannot proceed. If the respondent has completed and signed the consent, the applicant must complete the affidavit in part 3 of the form. This is sworn before a justice of the peace, a notary public or a commissioner for oaths after which the application is lodged with the sheriff clerk (see r 33.75 below).

(b) Five years' non-cohabitation

The procedure in this case is identical to that described above except that there is no need to obtain a signed consent from the respondent. When parts 1 and 2 have been completed, the application is lodged with the sheriff clerk.

A problem will arise if the respondent's address is unknown. In a two-year non-cohabitation case the application cannot proceed without the signed consent of the respondent. In five-year cases a remedy is provided in the rules (see r 33.77 below).

Lodging of applications (r 33.75)

Completed applications should be lodged (by post or by hand) with the sheriff clerk together with:

(i) an extract or certified copy of the marriage certificate; and

(ii) the appropriate fee.

The sheriff clerk will advise on the amount of the fee. In certain circumstances (explained in Form SP14), applicants may be exempted from payment of a fee, in which case Form SP15 should be completed. Both forms are available from the sheriff clerk.

Citation (r 33.76)

In simplified procedure citations or intimations are issued, in the first instance, by the sheriff clerk. Procedure varies depending on whether or not the address of the respondent is known.

(a) Address of respondent known

In both two-year and five-year cases a photocopy of the application is sent to the respondent together with a citation, in Form F34 and F35 depending on circumstances, advising him that the application has been lodged, that he may oppose it by putting reasons in writing and sending a letter to the sheriff clerk and that he may exercise a right to claim for financial provision.

The documents are sent by post and the envelope has the normal instructions regarding non-delivery printed on it (see page 20).

Service proceeds on a period of notice which commences on the day of posting. Where the period of notice expires on a Saturday, Sunday or public holiday, it is deemed to expire on the next day on which the sheriff clerk's office is open for civil court business.

The periods of notice are:

(i) where the defender is resident or has a place of business in Europe, twenty-one days after the date of execution of service; or

(ii) where the defender is resident or has a place of business outside Europe, forty-two days after the date of execution of service.

The sheriff may shorten or extend the period of notice but at least two days' notice must be given.

If postal service fails, the sheriff clerk may instruct service by sheriff officer. Before such instruction, the sheriff clerk will advise the applicant that, if the action is to proceed, service by officer is necessary and that a further fee must be paid in advance to the sheriff clerk by the applicant.

Service by officer may be personal or by leaving in the hands of an inmate or employee at the dwelling place or place of business. For service on persons furth of Scotland, see page 21.

Citation where address not known (r 33.77)

This situation may arise in five-year cases. If so, the applicant is directed, in the form, to:

(i) state the name, address and relationship of one of the next-of-kin of the respondent;

    (ii)   state the names, dates of birth and addresses of all children of the marriage.

A photocopy of the application and a notice in terms of Form F37 in the schedule to the rules are sent by post to the next-of-kin and children of the marriage whose addresses are known. If the addresses of the next-of-kin or children are unknown, a notice in terms of Form F36 is posted on the Walls of Court on a period of notice of twenty-one days.

Opposition to applications (r 33.78)

Any person who has been cited or to whom intimation has been made may:

    (i)   challenge the jurisdiction of the court; or

    (ii) oppose the grant of decree,

by letter, lodged within the period of notice, giving reasons for opposition. If there is opposition and the sheriff decides that it is not frivolous, the application must be dismissed. All decisions on opposition are intimated by the sheriff clerk to all parties concerned with the application. The lodging of a letter as described does not imply acceptance of the jurisdiction of the court.

Evidence (r 33.79)

Evidence in a simplified divorce application is given by affidavit. Parole evidence is not competent.

Decree

If the application is in order, the sheriff grants decree on the expiry of the period of notice. The sheriff clerk posts an extract of the decree in Form F38 to each party not sooner than fourteen days after the grant of decree.

If the application has been served in a country to which the 1965 Hague Convention applies (see page 21), the sheriff must also be satisfied that service has been effected in a way which conforms to the following conditions:

    (i)   the document was transmitted by one of the methods provided for in the Convention;

    (ii) a period of not less than six months (as may be considered adequate by the sheriff) has elapsed since the date of transmission of the document; and

    (iii) no certificate of any kind has been received even though every reasonable effort has been made to obtain it through the competent authorities of the state addressed.

Appeal (r 33.81)

A respondent may appeal against the interlocutor granting decree within fourteen days of the grant by addressing a letter to the court giving reasons for the appeal.

Applications after decree (r 33.82)

After the grant of decree, an application which could have been made if it had been made in an action of divorce must be made by minute.

Part XII — Variation of Court of Session decrees

Introduction

An award of aliment or one of the various orders all set out in s 8 of the Law Reform (Miscellaneous Provisions) (Scotland) Act 1966, made by the Court of Session, may be varied or recalled by the sheriff having jurisdiction over any party on whom an application for variation or recall has to be served.

Form of applications and intimation to the Court of Session (r 33.84)

Application is made by initial writ but, before lodging the initial writ with the sheriff clerk, a copy of the initial writ, certified as a true copy by the pursuer or his solicitor, must be lodged with, or sent by first class recorded delivery post to, the Deputy Principal Clerk of Session, to be lodged with the process of the cause in the Court of Session in which the original order was made.

The initial writ lodged with the sheriff clerk should have attached to it:

(i) a copy of the interlocutor, certified by a clerk of the Court of Session, which it is sought to vary; and

(ii) a certificate, by the pursuer or his solicitor, stating that a certified copy initial writ has been lodged with or sent to the Deputy Principal Clerk of Session, as described above.

If no notice of intention to defend is lodged, the action proceeds as an undefended family action, and decree may be pronounced after such enquiry as the sheriff thinks fit.

Defended actions (r 33.85)

Where a notice of intention to defend has been lodged and no request has been made to remit the application to the Court of Session (see below), the pursuer must, within fourteen days after the date of lodging of a notice of intention to defend, or within such other period as the sheriff may order, lodge in process the following documents (or copies) from the process in the cause in the Court of Session:

(i) the pleadings;

(ii) the interlocutor sheets;

(iii) any opinion of the court; and

(iv) any production on which he seeks to found,

and the sheriff may, at any time after the lodging of such documents:

(i) dispense with proof;

(ii) whether defences have been lodged or not, hear parties; and

(iii) thereafter grant decree or otherwise dispose of the cause as he thinks fit.

Transmission of process to the Court of Session (r 33.86)

Where decree has been granted or the cause otherwise disposed of, and the time for marking an appeal has expired, or an appeal having been marked has been disposed of, the sheriff clerk sends the sheriff court process and the Court of Session documents referred to above to the Court of Session; the sheriff court process then becomes part of the original Court of Session process.

Remit of applications to Court of Session (r 33.87)

Where a party has made an application in the sheriff court for variation or recall of a Court of Session decree (as described above), any other party to the action, not later than the first calling of the application in court, may request that the application be remitted to the Court of Session and, if such a request is made, the sheriff must remit the application.

The request must be made by motion and, within four days of the order remitting the application, the sheriff clerk sends the sheriff court process to the Court of Session where it becomes part of the original Court of Session process.

Part XIII — Child Support Act 1991

Restriction of expenses (r 33.89)

Where the Secretary of State is named as a defender in an action for declarator of non-parentage or illegitimacy (see page 99), and the Secretary of State does not defend the action, no expenses may be awarded against him.

Effect of maintenance assessments (r 33.90)

Where the sheriff clerk receives notification from the Child Support Agency that:

(i) a maintenance assessment has been made by the Agency which supersedes a decree or order in the sheriff court for aliment; or

(ii) a maintenance assessment has been cancelled,

the sheriff clerk must endorse on the interlocutor sheet of the process a certificate, in Form F39 or F40, as the case may be.

Effect of maintenance assessments on extracts relating to aliment (r 33.91)

Where an order relating to aliment is affected by a maintenance assessment, any extract of that order issued by the sheriff clerk must be endorsed with the following certificate:

'A maintenance assessment having been made under the Child Support Act 1991 on [date], this order, in so far as it relates to the making or securing periodical payments to or for the benefit of [names of children], ceases to have effect from [the date which is two days after the date on which the maintenance assessment was made]'.

Where an order relating to aliment has ceased to have effect on the making of a maintenance assessment, and that maintenance assessment is later cancelled or ceases to have effect, any extract of that order issued by the sheriff clerk must be endorsed also with the following certificate;

'The jurisdiction of the child support officer under the Child Support Act 1991 having terminated on [date], this order, in so far as it relates to [names of children], again shall have effect from [date of termination of child support officer's jurisdiction]'.

Chapter 36

Actions relating to heritable property

Part I — Sequestration for rent

Introduction

The purpose of an ordinary action of sequestration for rent is to enable the landlord to recover rent arrears and future rent due. Moveable articles are sequestrated and sold and the proceeds paid to the landlord. If there are insufficient articles in the premises to meet the amount due, the tenant may be ordered to replenish the premises (i.e. to furnish the premises with effects of sufficient value to afford the pursuer security for future rent due), failing which he may face ejection.

Actions craving payment for rent (r 34.1)

The action may be raised before or after the term of payment, and the writ normally includes craves for sequestration and sale:

   (i)   for non-payment of rent;

  (ii) for recovery of rent; or

 (iii) in security of rent.

A crave for an order to replenish if insufficient moveables are found in the premises is normally included along with a crave for ejection failing replenishment. The action proceeds in the normal manner.

Warrant to inventory and secure (r 34.2)

If the sheriff is satisfied that a *prima facie* case has been made out, the first warrant includes an order sequestrating the effects of the tenant and granting warrant to inventory and secure them. A copy of Form H1 is served with the initial writ and warrant of citation.

The procedure may include orders to sequestrate, to inventory and sell effects, to eject the tenant and to relet the premises. All of these orders include warrant to open shut and lockfast places.

Sale of effects (r 34.3)

The warrant of sale:

   (i)   will not be granted until the term for payment of rent has passed;

    (ii) authorises sale of so many of the effects as will meet the rent, interest and expenses;

   (iii) specifies where and when the sale will take place and the method of advertising the sale;

   (iv) directs the sale to proceed at the sight of a sheriff officer or other named person, e.g. an auctioneer.

The report of sale:

    (i) is lodged with the sheriff clerk by the pursuer within fourteen days of the sale; and

   (ii) includes the roup rolls, or certified copies, and a state of debt.

If there are surplus proceeds, these are lodged with the sheriff clerk and repaid to the tenant.

If there is a deficit, the pursuer may apply for a decree for the amount of deficit or for an order for the tenant to replenish the premises. If the tenant fails to replenish, the pursuer may apply for warrant to eject the tenant and to relet the premises.

Care of effects (r 34.4)

At any stage of the proceedings the sheriff may:

    (i) appoint a fit person to take charge of the sequestrated effects; or

   (ii) require the tenant to find caution (security) that they shall be made available.

Part II — Removing

Introduction

An ordinary action of removing is the process by which a tenant, whose right to occupancy has come to an end, is judicially warned to remove from the premises occupied by him, failing which he is liable to be ejected.

In this chapter, the term 'ejection' is used to describe the diligence following a decree of removing or the actual carrying out of the removing. This is distinct from an ordinary action of ejection, which is the process by which a person occupying heritable subjects without any right or title such as a squatter, is ejected therefrom. The 1907 Act also contains authority for ejection without recourse to the court (ss 34 and 35) and for warrant to eject without first obtaining a decree of removal (ss 36 and 37). These are classed as removings and are dealt with in this chapter.

A notice of removal (by the landlord) or letter of removal (by the tenant) is a prerequisite to an action of removing.

Actions of removing where fixed term of removal (r 34.5)

An ordinary action may be raised at any time provided:

(i) the tenant has bound himself to remove by writing, dated and signed within twelve months of the term of removal; or

(ii) where he has not so bound himself:

- in the case of a lease for three years and upwards, of lands exceeding two acres, not less than one year and not more than two years elapse between notice of removal and term of removal;

- in the case of the lease of such lands, written or oral from year to year or under tacit relocation or for less than three years, an interval of not less than six months elapses between notice of removal and term of removal; or

(iii) in the case of:

- houses with or without land not exceeding two acres;

- land not exceeding two acres without houses;

- mills, fishings and shootings; and

- all other heritable subjects excepting land exceeding two acres and let for one year or more;

forty days elapse between notice of removal and term of removal.

These provisions do not apply to subjects falling under the Agricultural Holdings (Scotland) Act 1949 of which s 24 has provision as to giving notice to quit.

In any defended ordinary action of removing, the sheriff may order the defender to find caution for violent profits, for example to cover damage done by the defender or the profit which the landlord could have made out of the subjects. If caution is ordered but not found, decree of removal may be pronounced forthwith.

In an action of irritancy and removing by a superior against a vassal, the pursuer must call as parties the last entered vassal and such heritable creditors and holders of postponed ground burdens as are disclosed by a search for twenty years prior to the action. The cost of the search forms part of the pursuer's expenses of process.

Removing without recourse to the court

(a) Probative lease (s 34 of the 1907 Act and r 34.6)

This procedure applies to land:

(i) which exceeds two acres; and

(ii) is held under a probative (presumed genuine without further proof) lease specifying a term of endurance.

Notice to remove must be in writing in terms of Form H2, and must be given:

(i) where the lease is for three years and upwards, not less than one year and not more than two years before the termination of the lease; and

(ii) in the case of leases from year to year, including lands occupied by tacit relocation, or for any period less than three years, not less than six months before the termination of the lease (or where there is a separate ish as regards land and houses or otherwise, before that ish which is first in date).

For the procedure for service and certification of notices to remove, see rr 34.8 and 34.9 below.

If the above conditions are satisfied, the lease, or an extract if it has been recorded in the books of court, has the same force and effect as a decree of removing obtained in an ordinary action. Written authority by the landlord, or anyone authorised by him, is sufficient warrant for a sheriff officer to eject the tenant and there being no decree, there is no need to serve a charge. The removal or ejection must be executed not later than six weeks from the date of the latest ish.

(b) Letter of removal (s 35 of the 1907 Act)

This procedure applies to lands which:

(i) exceed two acres;

(ii) are in the possession of a tenant, with or without a written lease; and where the tenant has signed a letter of removal (in terms of Form H3) at the date of entering or at any other time which is holograph or attested by one witness.

In these circumstances, the letter has the same force and effect as a decree of removing in an ordinary action. For the procedure for service and certification of the letter of removal, see rr 34.8 and 34.9 below.

If the above conditions are satisfied, the letter is sufficient warrant for ejection and can be implemented in the same manner and within the same time limit as in *(a)* above (probative lease).

Summary warrant

(a) Land exceeding two acres (s 36 of the 1907 Act)

This procedure applies in the case of lands exceeding two acres where:

(i) there is no written lease; and

(ii) no letter of removal has been granted by the tenant.

The tenancy may be ended by written notice, given by either side, not less than six months before the termination of the tenancy. The notice should be in terms of Form H2 or H3, as the case may be. If the tenant fails to remove, the landlord may apply to the court for a summary warrant of ejection. This is an ordinary action and the normal rules of procedure apply.

(b) Lands let for a year or more (s 37 of the 1907 Act)

In cases of:

(i)   houses, with or without land attached not exceeding two acres;

(ii) lands not exceeding two acres let without houses;

(iii) mills, fishings and shootings;

(iv) all other heritable subjects excepting land exceeding two acres,

let for a year or more, notice of termination of the tenancy may be given by one or other of the parties. Notice in terms of Form H3 or H4, as the case may be, must be given at least forty days before:

(i)   the fifteenth day of May when the termination of the tenancy is the term of Whit-Sunday; or

(ii) the eleventh day of November when the termination is the term of Martinmas.

If the tenant fails to remove, the landlord may apply to the court for a warrant of summary ejection. This is an ordinary action and the normal rules of procedure apply.

Giving notice of removal (r 34.8)

Removal notices under s 34, 35, 36 or 37 of the 1907 Act may be given by:

(i)   a sheriff officer; or

(ii) registered letter or first class recorded delivery post by the person entitled to give notice, or the solicitor or factor of such person.

The notice, if posted, must be posted in time to admit of its being delivered at or prior to the last date on which notice must be given. It should be addressed to the person entitled to receive it and should bear his particular address at the time, if known, or, if not known, his last known address.

Evidence of notice to remove (r 34.9)

(a) Lease or letter of removal

The following constitute sufficient evidence that notice has been given:

(i)   a certificate that notice has been given in cases under s 34, 35, 36 or 37 endorsed on:

• the lease or extract; or

• the letter of removal

by the sheriff officer, person giving notice or the solicitor or factor of such person; or

(ii) an acknowledgment of notice endorsed as above, by the party in possession or his agent.

(b) No lease or letter of removal

A certificate endorsed on a copy notice or letter (certified correct) by the person, sheriff officer, solicitor or factor sending the notice or letter and signed by such party is sufficient evidence that notice has been given.

Applications under Part II of the Conveyancing and Feudal Reform (Scotland) Act 1970 (r 34.10)

Applications or counter-applications under the above Act normally proceed as summary applications. However, an application or counter-application under any of the following sections must be made by initial writ, and follow ordinary cause procedure, where any other remedy is craved:

(i) s 18(2) (declarator that obligations under a contract have been performed);

(ii) s 20(3) (application by a creditor for a warrant to let security subjects);

(iii) s 22(1) objections to notice of default);

(iv) s 22(3) (counter-application for remedies under the Act);

(v) s 24(1) (application by a creditor for a warrant to exercise remedies on default); and

(vi) s 28(1) (decree of foreclosure).

An interlocutor of the sheriff disposing of an application or counter-application proceeding under ordinary cause procedure is final and not subject to appeal except as to a question of title or any other remedy granted.

Chapter 37

Actions of multiplepoinding

Introduction

The purpose of an action of multiplepoinding is to determine the rights in a fund or subject, known as the fund *in medio*, on which there are two or more competing claims.

The fund *in medio* may consist of moveables, moveable rights, heritage or heritable rights. It often consists of money.

The action may be raised by the holder of the fund, who asks the court to decide how the fund should be distributed or by a claimant on the fund whose claim has been refused by the holder.

Parties (r 35.3)

The holder of the fund should be identified in the instance of the initial writ as follows:

(i) if the holder of the fund raises the action, the instance should read: 'AB (*design*) holder of the fund *in medio*, Pursuer'; or

(ii) if a claimant on the fund raises the action, the instance should read:
'CD (*design*) claimant on the fund *in medio*, Pursuer against EF (*design*) holder of the fund *in medio*, Defender'.

Condescendence of fund *in medio* (r 35.4)

All known claimants on the fund or other interested parties should be called as defenders.

If the pursuer is the holder of the fund, the condescendence of the initial writ should contain a detailed description of the fund *in medio*.

If the holder of the fund is not the pursuer, the holder must, before the expiry of the period of notice:

(i) lodge in process:
- a condescendence of the fund *in medio*, stating any claim or lien which he may profess to have on the fund;
- a list of all persons known to him as having an interest in the fund; and

(ii) intimate a copy of the condescendence and list to any other party.

Warrant of citation in multiplepoindings (r 35.5)

The warrant to cite is in Form M1.

Citation (r 35.6)

Citation is in Form M2 with a copy of the initial writ and Form M4, and service is ordered on all parties known to have an interest in the fund (this will generally mean the defenders), including the holder of the fund where the pursuer is not the holder. (For service on a person whose address is not known, see page 23.)

A certificate of citation in Form M3 is attached to the initial writ.

Advertisement (r 35.7)

It is possible that there will be unknown claimants on the fund, and, to cover this, the sheriff may include in the warrant to cite a direction that the import of the initial writ should be advertised in such newspapers as he considers necessary.

Lodging of notice of appearance (r 35.8)

Where a party intends to lodge:

(i)   defences to the competency of the action;

(ii) objections to the condescendence of the fund *in medio* (if this has been included in the initial writ); or

(iii) a claim on the fund,

he must, before the expiry of the period of notice, lodge a notice of appearance (not a notice of intention to defend) in Form M4.

Fixing the date of the first hearing (r 35.9)

Where:

(i)   a notice of appearance; or

(ii) a condescendence of the fund *in medio* and list (where the pursuer is not the holder of the fund),

has been lodged, the sheriff clerk must prepare and sign an interlocutor fixing a date and time for the first hearing, to be held not sooner than four weeks after the expiry of the period of notice, and intimate the date of the hearing, in Form M5, to each party.

Hearings (r 35.10)

At the first hearing, an assessment is made by the sheriff of the various interests of the parties who have entered appearance. The sheriff appoints a period within which defences, objections or claims must be lodged, and fixes a date for a second hearing.

If the list lodged by the holder (referred to above) contains the name of any person who is not a party to the action, the sheriff orders:

(i) the initial writ to be amended to add that person as a defender;

(ii) service of the amended pleadings on that person with a citation in Form M6; and

(iii) intimation to that person of any condescendence of the fund *in medio* lodged by a holder of the fund who is not the pursuer,

and if the person on whom service is made lodges a notice of appearance, the sheriff clerk intimates to him, in Form M5, the date of the next hearing fixed in the action.

Lodging defences, objections and claims (r 35.11)

Defences, objections and claims may be combined in one document under separate headings, and should be accompanied by any document founded on, if within the custody or power of the claimant.

Disposal of defences (r 35.12)

If defences have been lodged, they must be disposed of before the action can proceed. The sheriff fixes a period for the adjustment of the initial writ and the defences, after which the record is closed and the action proceeds as directed by the sheriff.

If no defences have been lodged, or having been lodged they have been disposed of, the next stage in the procedure concerns objections to the fund *in medio*.

Objections to fund *in medio* (r 35.13)

If objections have been lodged, the sheriff fixes a period for the adjustment of the condescendence of the fund and objections after which the record is closed and the action proceeds as an ordinary cause.

If no objections have been lodged, or having been lodged they have been disposed of, the sheriff, without order for intimation to any other party, may, on the motion of the holder of the fund, approve the condescendence of the fund and find the holder liable only in once and single payment.

Preliminary pleas in multiplepoindings (r 35.14)

The procedure for dealing with preliminary pleas in multiplepoindings is similar to that in ordinary actions in general. A note of the basis of the plea must be lodged with the sheriff clerk not later than three days before the hearing to determine further procedure, failing which he is deemed to be no longer insisting on the plea which will be repelled by the sheriff. If the plea is sustained, the sheriff appoints the action to debate.

Consignation of the fund and discharge of the holder (r 35.15)

The sheriff, having approved the condescendence of the fund *in medio*, may order it to be consigned or deposited with the sheriff clerk. If the fund or part of it is not easily divisible, the sheriff may order the whole or part of the fund to be sold and the proceeds consigned with the sheriff clerk.

When the holder has consigned or deposited the fund, he may apply for his exoneration and discharge and when this has been granted, the sheriff may allow the holder his expenses out of the fund as a first charge on it.

Further service or advertisement (r 35.16)

At this stage the fund has been consigned, but before ordering division and payment, the sheriff may order further advertisement or service on any person if it is doubtful if all possible claimants are aware of the action.

Ranking of claims (r 35.17)

When the holder of the fund has been exonerated and discharged and has consigned the fund he is no longer involved in the process. The next stage is to decide how the fund should be divided among the claimants.

Claims may be lodged at a late stage in the proceedings (see r 35.16 above). If all claimants are agreed on the division of the fund the sheriff will rank and prefer claimants in terms of their claims. However, if there is competition among claimants, the sheriff fixes a period for the adjustment of claims after which the record is closed, and the sheriff will then fix a date for a hearing on claims or he will remit the case to a reporter (see below).

Remit to reporter (r 35.18)

If he considers it to be necessary, the sheriff may remit the case to a reporter to prepare a scheme of division and report back. The expenses of the remit, when approved by the sheriff, are a charge on the fund to be deducted before division.

Final procedure

Before making payment to claimants, the sheriff clerk may require the exhibition of tax clearance certificates (see page 89).

Chapter 38

Actions of damages

Part I — Intimation to connected persons in certain actions of damages

Introduction

This part applies to an action in which, following the death of any person from personal injuries, damages are claimed by:

(i)   the executor of the deceased, in respect of the injuries from which the deceased died; or

(ii) any relative of the deceased, in respect of the death of the deceased.

Where there is a possibility of separate actions being raised by claimants against the same defender, the rules provide that, in the event of an action being raised, notice must be given to all possible claimants where practicable so that, in the interest of reducing expense, all claims may be brought in a single action.

'Relative', as defined in the Damages (Scotland) Act 1976, includes:

(i)   the spouse of the deceased;

(ii) any person who was living with the deceased as husband or wife;

(iii) a parent or child of the deceased;

(iv) any person who was accepted by the deceased as a child of his family;

(v)   any ascendant or descendant (other than a parent or child) of the deceased; and

(vi) any person who, having been a spouse of the deceased, has ceased to be so by virtue of a divorce.

Any person, not being a party to the action, who has title to sue the defender in respect of the personal injuries from which the deceased died or in respect of his death, is referred to in the rules as a 'connected person'.

Averments (r 36.2)

There is an onus on the pursuer to state in the condescendence:

(i)   that there are no connected persons (or that he is the only person with a title to sue the defender); or

(ii) that there are connected persons (in which case the pursuer must name and give the designation of such persons); or

(iii) that there are connected persons in respect of whom intimation should be dispensed with on the grounds that:

- the names or whereabouts of such persons are not known to the pursuer and cannot be reasonably ascertained; or
- such persons are unlikely to be awarded more than £200 each.

Warrants for intimation (r 36.3)

If any connected person is specifically identified in the condescendence, the initial writ must include a crave for intimation to such person, and such intimation is given in Form D1 with a copy of the initial writ.

Applications to dispense with intimation (r 36.4)

Where the pursuer avers that intimation should be dispensed with for the reasons mentioned above, he should include a crave in the initial writ for an order to dispense with intimation.

The initial writ is considered by the sheriff who must have regard on the one hand to the need to avoid a multiplicity of actions relating to the same circumstances, and the expense and difficulty of taking steps to ascertain the name and whereabouts of connected persons, and, on the other hand, to ensuring that due consideration is given to the interests of such persons.

If not satisfied that intimation should be dispensed with, the sheriff may order such intimation, further enquiry or advertisement as he deems appropriate.

Subsequent disclosure of connected person (r 36.5)

Where the sheriff has dispensed with intimation to a connected person, whose name or whereabouts subsequently become known to the pursuer, the pursuer must apply, by motion, for a warrant for intimation to such person and, if granted, a notice of intimation in Form D1 and a copy of the initial writ is served on such person.

Connected persons entering process (r 36.6)

Any connected person who is not a party to the action may apply, by minute, to be sisted as an additional pursuer. The minute must crave leave to adopt the existing grounds of the action and to make appropriate amendments to the crave, condescendence and pleas-in-law of the initial writ.

The normal procedure for dealing with minutes does not apply, except for the procedure on intimation, opposition and hearing of motions. The minute must be intimated to all other parties who are given fourteen days from the date of intimation to lodge answers.

Failure to enter process (r 36.7)

Any connected person who receives intimation of the action may opt to raise a separate action rather than be sisted as an additional pursuer in an existing action but, in that event, he would not be awarded the expenses of that action, except on cause shown.

Part II — Interim payments of damages

Applications for interim payment of damages (r 36.9)

An order for an interim payment in an action of damages for personal injury or the death of a person in consequence of personal injuries may be made on an admission of liability by the defender, or if the sheriff is satisfied, on an assessment of the written pleadings and having heard parties, that the pursuer would be successful. Certain conditions have to be satisfied before an order for interim payment may be made.

In any action for damages for personal injury or the death of a person in consequence of personal injuries, the pursuer may at any time after the lodging of defences, apply for an interim payment of damages. The application is made by written motion served on the defender(s) and any other party on a period of notice of fourteen days.

If, after hearing parties on the motion, the sheriff is satisfied either:

(i)   that the defender(s) has admitted liability; or

(ii) that, if the action proceeded to proof, the pursuer would succeed on the question of liability without a substantial finding of contributory negligence and would obtain decree for damages,

and that the defender is:

(i)   insured in respect of the pursuer's claim;

(ii) a public authority; or

(iii) a person whose means and resources are such as to enable him to make an interim payment,

he may order the defender to make an interim payment to the pursuer of such an amount, not exceeding such reasonable proportion of the damages which in the opinion of the sheriff is likely to be recovered by the pursuer, as he deems appropriate.

Payment may be ordered in a lump sum or otherwise and is subject to the provisions of Part IV (management of damages payable to persons under a legal disability — see below). A second or subsequent application may be made on cause shown by reason of a change of circumstances.

The above provisions also apply to a counterclaim for damages for personal injury made by a defender.

'Personal injuries' include any disease or impairment of a person's physical or mental condition.

Adjustment on final decree (r 36.10)

Any interim payment made under the above provisions is taken into account when the sheriff is giving effect to the defender's liability to the pursuer.

The pursuer may be ordered to repay to the defender any sum by which the interim payment exceeds the amount which the defender is liable to pay to the pursuer.

The sheriff may order any other defender or third party to make payment of any part of the interim payment which the defender who made it is entitled to recover from that other defender or third party by way of contribution or indemnity or in respect of any remedy or relief related to or connected with the pursuer's claim.

Part III — Provisional damages for personal injuries

Introduction

Section 12 of the Administration of Justice Act 1982 applies to actions for damages for personal injuries in which:

(i) there is proved or admitted to be a risk that at some definite or indefinite time in the future the injured person will, as the result of the act or omission which gave rise to the cause of the action, develop some serious disease or suffer some serious deterioration in his physical or mental condition; and

(ii) the responsible person was, at the time of the act or omission giving rise to the cause of the action,

• a public authority or public corporation; or

• insured or otherwise indemnified in respect of the claim.

Applications for provisional damages (r 36.12)

Applications for provisional damages are made by including in the initial writ:

(i) a crave for provisional damages;
(ii) averments in the condescendence supporting the crave and averments in line with the provisions in s 12 relating to risk and the responsible person; and
(iii) an appropriate plea-in-law.

If the crave is granted, the sheriff may award provisional damages assessed on the assumption that the injured person will not develop the disease or suffer the deterioration in his condition.

Applications for further damages (r 36.13)

If, in applying for provisional damages (see r 36.12), the injured person has also applied for and been granted an order authorising him to apply for further damages, application for further damages is made by minute in the process to which it relates and must include:

(i)   a crave for further damages;

(ii) averments in the statement of facts supporting the crave; and

(iii) appropriate pleas-in-law,

and be accompanied by a motion for warrant to serve the minute on:

(i)   every other party; and

(ii) where such other party is insured or otherwise indemnified, his insurer or indemnifier, if known to the pursuer,

and any such party, insurer or indemnifier may lodge answers within twenty-eight days after the date of service.

Where answers have been lodged, the sheriff may, on the motion of any party, make such order as to procedure as he thinks fit.

Part IV — Management of damages payable to persons under a legal disability

Orders for payment and management of money (r 36.14)

This rule operates where a court has granted decree, or there has been an extra-judicial settlement, in an action for damages and a sum of money is payable to a person under a legal disability. A typical case is where a father has been fatally injured in the course of his employment and his minor or pupil children have been awarded damages.

The sheriff may make such order regarding the payment and management of such a sum for the benefit of such person as he thinks fit.

Methods of management (r 36.15)

In making a management order, the sheriff may:

(i)   appoint a judicial factor to apply, invest or deal with the money;

(ii) order the money to be paid to:
  • the Accountant of Court; or
  • the guardian of the person under a legal disability; or

(iii) order the money to be paid to the sheriff clerk of the district in which the person under a legal disability resides.

All of these options have as their objective the need to look after the interests of the person under legal disability but, instead of applying one of the above methods, the sheriff may order the money to be paid directly to the person under legal disability.

Subsequent orders (r 36.16)

Where the sheriff has made an order for payment and management, any person having an interest may apply, by minute, for a change of order or for a change in the directions of the sheriff on how the money should be applied, invested or otherwise dealt with by the Accountant of Court, guardian or sheriff clerk as the case may be.

Management of money paid to sheriff clerk (r 36.17)

A receipt in Form D2 by the sheriff clerk is sufficient discharge in respect of money paid to him either following an action in his own court or at the request of another court.

Investment of the money by the sheriff clerk is restricted to the way in which trustees are authorised to invest money by virtue of the Trustee Investment Act 1961.

The money is paid out or applied for the benefit of the entitled person as the sheriff may direct. Payments may be regular for fixed amounts, occasional for specific purposes, or no requests for payments may be received. When the entitled person is no longer under legal disability (usually when he attains the age of sixteen), the money is paid over to him, on his application.

Part V — Sex Discrimination Act 1975

Introduction

An action which alleges a breach of statutory duty under s 66(1) of the Sex Discrimination Act 1975 will normally include a claim for reparation, and so will proceed as an ordinary action. However, proceedings must not be instituted unless the claimant has given notice of the claim to the Secretary of State (the Equal Opportunities Commission) and:

(i) the Secretary of State has by notice informed the claimant that he does not require further time to consider the matter; or

(ii) the period of two months has elapsed since the claimant gave notice to the Secretary of State.

Causes under section 66 of the 1975 Act (r 36.18)

Having raised an action under s 66 of the Act, the pursuer should send a copy of the initial writ to the Equal Opportunities Commission by first class recorded delivery post.

The sheriff may, of his own motion or on the motion of any party, appoint a person who the sheriff considers has special qualifications to be of assistance in determining the action, as an assessor.

Chapter 39

Causes under the Presumption of Death (Scotland) Act 1977

Introduction

Where a person who is missing is thought to have died, or has not been known to be alive, for a period of at least seven years, any person having an interest may raise an action of declarator of the death of that person. The usual reason for raising an action under the Act is so that the estate may be appropriated by those who would have taken it in the event of the missing person having actually died at the date found by the court to be the date of death or the presumed date of death.

The sheriff court has jurisdiction to entertain an action of declarator under the Act if:

(i) the missing person:

- was domiciled in Scotland on the date on which he was last known to be alive; or
- had been habitually resident in Scotland throughout the period of one year ending with that date; and

(ii) the missing person's last known place of residence in Scotland was in the sheriffdom;

or

(iii) the pursuer in the action:

- is the spouse of the missing person; and
- is domiciled in Scotland at the date of raising the action or was habitually resident there throughout the period of one year ending with that date, and was resident in the sheriffdom for a period of not less than forty days ending with the date of raising the action.

Parties to, and service and intimation of, actions of declarator (r 37.2)

The missing person is named as the defender in the instance of the initial writ which must include a crave for a warrant for intimation to:

(i) the missing person's:

- spouse; and
- children or, if he has no children, his nearest relative known to the pursuer;

(ii) any person, including any insurance company, who so far as is known to the pursuer has an interest; and

(iii) the Lord Advocate,

in the following terms:

'For intimation to [*name and address*] as [husband or wife, child or nearest relative] [a person having an interest in the presumed death] of [*name and address of the missing person*] and to the Lord Advocate'.

Service on the missing person is executed in the same way as for service on a person whose address is not known (see page 23), except that Form P1 is used instead of G3.

Intimation on the persons mentioned at (i) and (ii) above may, on the motion of the pursuer, be dispensed with by the sheriff but, where intimation is required, a copy of the initial writ and Form P2 are served in the usual way (see Chapter 7).

Any person having an interest may lodge a minute craving the making by the court of any determination or appointment not sought by the pursuer, in which case the minute should contain an appropriate crave, condescendence and plea-in-law. A copy of the minute must be sent, by registered post or first class recorded delivery service, to each person who has been served with a copy initial writ, after which the minute is lodged with the sheriff clerk with the relevant Post Office receipts or certificates of posting.

Further advertisement (r 37.3)

If the sheriff considers it necessary, he may, of his own motion or on the motion of a party, order such further advertisement as he thinks fit.

Applications for proof (r 37.4)

When all orders for service, intimation and advertisement (if any) have been complied with, the pursuer must apply, by motion, for an order for proof. The motion is intimated in the usual way (see page 48), and proof is by affidavit evidence unless the sheriff otherwise directs.

The sheriff, having considered the evidence and being satisfied on a balance of probabilities that the missing person:

(i) has died, grants decree accordingly and includes a finding as to the date and time of death. If it is uncertain when, within any period of time, the missing person died, the sheriff finds that he died at the end of that period; or

(ii) has not been known to be alive for a period of at least seven years, grants decree and includes a finding that the missing person died at the end of the day occurring seven years after the date on which he was last known to be alive.

Applications for variation or recall of a decree (r 37.5)

Decree may, on application made at any time by any person having an interest, be varied or recalled by the court which granted the decree. Application is made by minute and the sheriff makes an order:

(i) for service on the 'missing person' where his whereabouts have become known;

(ii) for intimation on the persons on whom intimation was made when the initial writ was first lodged, unless the sheriff dispenses with such intimation; and

(iii) for any answers to be lodged within such period as the sheriff thinks fit.

If an application to vary the decree is lodged, any person having an interest and who seeks a determination or appointment which has not been sought by the person applying for the variation order, may, by lodging answers to the application, crave the court to make the determination or appointment sought.

The person lodging the answers must:

(i) send a copy of the answers to the minuter;

(ii) send a copy of the answers by registered post or first class recorded delivery service to each person on whom service or intimation of the minute was ordered; and

(iii) lodge in process the Post Office receipt or certificate of posting.

Appointment of judicial factors (r 37.6)

Any person having an interest may lodge a minute seeking the appointment of a judicial factor on the estate of the missing person. In granting decree of declarator, the sheriff may also appoint a judicial factor, in which case the Act of Sederunt (Judicial Factors Rules) 1992 applies.

Chapter 40

The European Court

Introduction

This chapter applies to references to the Court of Justice of the European Communities for preliminary rulings:

(i) under art 177 of the European Economic Community Treaty;

(ii) under art 150 of the European Atomic Energy Community Treaty;

(iii) under art 41 of the European Coal and Steel Community Treaty; or

(iv) on the conventions as defined in s 1(1) of the Civil Jurisdiction and Judgments Act 1982, under art 3 of Sch 2 to that Act.

Applications for reference (r 38.2)

A reference may be made by the sheriff *ex proprio motu*, or on the motion of any party to the proceedings, for a preliminary ruling on the interpretation of the treaties or the interpretation, validity etc of acts, statutes or institutions established under the treaties, where such interpretation, validity etc is in issue in the proceedings before the sheriff. The reference is made in Form E1.

Preparation of case for reference (r 38.3)

When the sheriff has decided that a reference should be made, the case is continued *simpliciter* and the sheriff drafts a reference within four weeks.

The sheriff clerk sends a copy of the draft reference to each party.

Within four weeks of the issue of the draft reference, each party may lodge adjustments with the sheriff clerk and, at the same time, send a copy to each of the other parties.

Within fourteen days after the latest date on which adjustments either are or could be lodged the sheriff, after considering any adjustments, must make and sign the reference and this step is intimated to the parties by the sheriff clerk.

Sist of cause (r 38.4)

Unless the sheriff otherwise orders, procedure in the action is sisted until the European Court has given a preliminary ruling, but the sheriff may recall the sist to make any interim order which a due regard to the interests of the parties may require.

Transmission of reference (r 38.5)

Provided that no appeal procedure is involved (see below), a copy of the reference, certified by the sheriff clerk, is transmitted by the sheriff clerk to the Registrar of the European Court.

Unless the sheriff otherwise directs, a reference shall not be sent to the European Court if:

(i)   the time for applying for leave to appeal or for marking an appeal has not expired; or

(ii) an appeal having been marked has not been disposed of.

Appendices: Contents

Appendix 1: Forms

155

Appendix 2: Forms for extract decrees

It is acknowledged that the forms reproduced in the Appendices are Crown copyright.

Appendix 1

Forms

FORM G1   Rule 3.1(1)

Form of initial writ

INITIAL WRIT

SHERIFFDOM OF (*insert name of sheriffdom*)
AT (*insert place of sheriff court*)

[A.B.] (*design and state any special capacity in which the pursuer is suing*).
Pursuer.

Against

[C.D.] (*design and state any special capacity in which the defender is being sued*).
Defender.

The Pursuer craves the court (*here state the specific decree, warrant or order sought*).

CONDESCENDENCE
(*State in numbered paragraphs the facts which form the ground of action*)

PLEAS-IN-LAW
(*State in numbered sentences*)

Signed
[A.B.], Pursuer.
or [X.Y.], Solicitor for the pursuer (*state designation and business address*)

FORM G2   Rule 4.2(1)

Form of caveat

SHERIFFDOM OF (*insert name of sheriffdom*)
AT (*insert place of sheriff court*)

CAVEAT for [A.B.] (*insert designation and address**)

Should any application be made for (*here specify the nature of the application(s) to which this caveat is to apply*) before the lodging of a notice of intention to defend, it is requested that intimation be made to the caveator before any order is pronounced.

Date (*insert date*)   Signed
                                    [A.B.]
                                    or [X.Y.] Solicitor for [A.B.] (*add designation and business address*)

Caveator's telephone and fax number (*insert where caveat is not lodged by solicitor*)

Solicitor (*insert name and address, telephone and fax number and reference*)

Out of hours contacts:
       1. (*insert name and telephone number*)
       2. (*insert name and telephone number*)

*State whether the caveat is lodged in an individual capacity, or a specified representative capacity (e.g. as trustee of a named trust) or both. Where appropriate, state also the nature of the caveator's interest (e.g. shareholder, debenture holder).

FORM G3   Rule 5.6(1)(a)

Form of advertisement

NOTICE TO [C.D.]   Court ref.no.
An action has been raised in   Sheriff Court by [A.B.], Pursuer, calling as a Defender [C.D.] whose last known address was (*insert last known address of defender*). If [C.D.] wishes to defend the action [*where notice is given in a family action add:* or make any claim or seek any order] he [*or* she] should immediately contact the sheriff clerk at (*insert address*) from whom the service copy initial writ may be obtained. If he [*or* she] fails to do so decree may be granted against him [*or* her].

        Signed
          [X.Y.], (*add designation and business address*)
          Solicitor for the pursuer
          or [P.Q.], (*add business address*)
          Sheriff officer

FORM G4   Rules 5.6(1)(b) and 33.16(3)(b)

Form of notice for walls of court

NOTICE TO [C.D.]   Court ref.no.
An action has been raised in   Sheriff Court by [A.B.], Pursuer, calling
as a Defender [C.D.] whose last known address was (*insert last known address of defender*). If [C.D.] wishes to defend the action [*where notice is to be given in a family action add*: or make any claim or seek any order] he [*or* she] should immediately contact the sheriff clerk at (*insert address*) from whom the service copy initial writ may be obtained. If he [*or* she] fails to do so decree may be granted against him [*or* her].

Date (*insert date*)   Signed
                            Sheriff clerk (depute)
                            Telephone no. (*insert telephone number of sheriff clerk's office*)

FORM G5   Rules 9.2(2)(a) and 33.16(3)(b)

Form of intimation of Options Hearing

Sheriff Court (*insert address and telephone number*)   Court ref.no.

[A.B.] (*design*) Pursuer against [C.D.] (*design*) Defender

You are given notice that in this action:-

| (*insert date*) | is the last day for lodging defences; |

| (*insert date*) | is the last day for making adjustments to the writ or defences; |

| (*insert date, time and place*) | is the date, time and place for the Options Hearing. |

Date (*insert date*)   Signed
                                            Sheriff clerk (depute)

NOTE:
If you fail to comply with the terms of this notice or with any of the rules 9.3, 9.4, 9.6, 9.10, and 9.11 of the Standard Procedure of the Ordinary Cause Rules of the Sheriff Court, decree by default may be granted in terms of rule 16.2(2) of those Rules.

(*continued*)

Appendix 1

NOTE TO BE ADDED WHERE PARTY UNREPRESENTED

NOTE
IF YOU ARE UNCERTAIN WHAT ACTION TO TAKE you should consult a solicitor. You may be eligible for legal aid depending on your income, and you can get information from any Citizens Advice Bureau or other advice agency.

Form G6   Rule 15.1(1)(b)

Form of motion

SHERIFFDOM OF (*insert name of sheriffdom*)   Court ref.no.
AT (*insert place of sheriff court*)

MOTION FOR THE PURSUER [*or* DEFENDER]
in the cause
[A.B.] (*insert designation and address*)
Pursuer
against
[C.D.] (*insert designation and address*)
Defender

The (*insert description of party*) moves the court to (*insert details of motion and, where appropriate, the reason(s) for seeking the order*).

List the documents or parts of process lodged with the motion:-
(*Insert description of document or name part of process*)

Date (*insert date*)   Signed
Party (*insert name and description of party*)
or Solicitor for party
(*insert designation and business address*)

Form G7   Rule 15.2(1)

Form of intimation of motion

SHERIFFDOM OF (*insert name of sheriffdom*)   Court ref.no.
AT (*insert place of sheriff court*)
in the cause

[A.B.] (*insert designation and address*)
Pursuer
against
[C.D.] (*insert designation and address*)
Defender

(1) Date fixed for hearing motion (*insert date and time*)

(2) Last date for lodging notice of opposition (*insert date*)

APPLICATION IS MADE BY MOTION FOR THE ORDER(S) SOUGHT IN THE ATTACHED FORM (*attach a copy of Form G6*)

*A copy of the document(s) or part(s) of process referred to in Form G6 is attached.

OPPOSITION TO THE MOTION MAY BE MADE by completing Form G9 (notice of opposition to motion) and lodging it with the sheriff clerk at (*insert address*) on or before (*insert date for lodging the notice of opposition*). In that event the motion will be called in court (*insert date and time fixed for hearing motion*). A copy of the notice of opposition must be sent immediately to any other party in the action.

IF NO NOTICE OF OPPOSITION IS LODGED, the motion may be considered by the sheriff without the attendance of parties.

Date (*insert date*)   Signed

Party (*insert name and
description of party*)
or Solicitor for party
(*insert designation and business
address*)

*Delete as appropriate.

EXPLANATORY NOTE TO BE ADDED WHERE PARTY TO WHOM INTIMATION IS MADE IS NOT LEGALLY REPRESENTED

IF YOU ARE UNCERTAIN WHAT ACTION TO TAKE you should consult a solicitor. You may also receive advice from a Citizens Advice Bureau or other advice agency.

(*continued*)

NOTE
If you intend to oppose the motion you must appear or be represented on the date of the hearing. If you return Form G9 (notice of opposition to motion) and then fail to attend or be represented at the court hearing, the court may consider the motion in your absence and may grant the order(s) sought.

Form G8   Rule 15.2(6)

Form of certificate of intimation of motion

CERTIFICATE OF INTIMATION OF MOTION

I certify that intimation of the motion was made to (*insert names of parties or solicitors for the parties, as appropriate*) by (*insert method of intimation; where intimation is by facsimile transmission, insert fax number to which intimation sent*) on (*insert date of intimation*).

Date (*insert date*)   Signed

           Solicitor *or*
           Sheriff officer
           (*add designation and business address*)

Form G9   Rule 15.3(1)(a)

Form of notice of opposition to motion

NOTICE OF OPPOSITION TO MOTION

SHERIFFDOM OF (*insert name of sheriffdom*)   Court ref.no.
AT (*insert place of sheriff court*)
           in the cause
[A.B.] (*insert designation and address*)
                Pursuer
         against
[C.D.] (*insert designation and address*)
                Defender

Date and time for hearing of motion (*insert date and time*)

Notice of opposition to motion given by (*insert name of party opposing motion*) on (*insert date of lodging of notice of opposition with sheriff clerk*)

Intimation of notice of opposition sent to (*insert name of party*)
on (*insert date*)
by (*insert method of intimation; where intimation is made by facsimile transmission, insert fax number to which notice of opposition sent*)

Date (*insert date*)   Signed

Party (*insert name and designation of party*)
or Solicitor for party (*add designation and business address*)

Form G10   Rule 24.2(3)

Form of intimation to a party whose solicitor has withdrawn

SHERIFFDOM OF (*insert name of sheriffdom*)
AT (*insert place of sheriff court*)

in the cause
[A.B.], (*insert designation*),

Pursuer

against
[C.D.], (*insert designation*)

Defender

Court ref.no.

The court has been informed that your solicitors have ceased to act for you.

As a result the sheriff has ordered that you appear or be represented on (*insert date and time*) within the Sheriff Court at the above address. A copy of the order is attached.

When you appear you will be asked by the sheriff to state whether you intend to proceed with your action [*or* defences *or* answers].

Date (*insert date*)   Signed

Solicitor (*add designation and business address*)

NOTE:
IF YOU ARE UNCERTAIN WHAT ACTION TO TAKE you should consult a solicitor. You may also obtain advice from any Citizens Advice Bureau or other advice agency.

FORM G11   Rule 28.3(1)

Form of notice in optional procedure for commission and diligence

Order by the Sheriff Court at (*insert address*)   Court ref.no.

In the cause

[A.B.](*design*) Pursuer

against

[C.D.] (*design*) Defender

To (*insert name and designation of party or parties or haver, from whom documents are sought to be recovered*)

You are given notice that you are required to produce to the sheriff clerk at the above address within seven days of (*insert date on which service was executed. N.B. Rule 5.3(2) relating to postal service or intimation*):

    (1) this order; which must be produced intact;

    (2) a certificate signed and completed in terms of the form appended to this notice; and

    (3) all documents in your possession falling within the enclosed specification, with an inventory of such documents signed by you relating to this order and your certificate.

Production may be made by lodging the documents with the sheriff clerk at the above address, by posting them by registered post or the first class recorded delivery service addressed to the sheriff clerk at the above address.

Date (*insert date*)   Signed

Solicitor for party (*add designation and business address of the solicitor for the party in whose favour commission and diligence granted*)

NOTE

If you claim confidentiality for any of the documents produced by you, such documents must nevertheless be produced, but may be placed in a special sealed packet by themselves, marked "confidential".

. . . .

CERTIFICATE

I hereby certify with reference to the order of the Sheriff Court at (*insert place of sheriff court*) in the cause (*insert court ref. no.*) and the relative specification of documents, served upon me and marked respectively X and Y:

(1) that the documents which are produced and which are numbered in the inventory signed by me and marked Z, are the whole documents in my possession falling under the specification [*or* that I have no documents in my possession falling within the specification].

(2) that, to the best of my knowledge and belief, there are in existence other documents falling within the specification, but not in my possession, namely (*describe them by reference to one or more of the descriptions of documents in the specification*), which were last seen by me on or about (*insert date*), at (*insert place*), in the hands of (*insert name and address of the person*) [*or* that I know of the existence of no documents in the possession of any person, other than myself, which fall within the specification].

Signed

FORM G12   Rules 28.3(3) and 29.7(4)

Form of certificate of citation of witness or haver

I certify that on (*insert date of citation*)   I duly cited [K.L.], (*design*) to attend at (*insert name of sheriff court*) Sheriff Court on (*insert date*) at (*insert time*) as a witness for the pursuer [*or* defender] in the action at the instance of [A.B.] (*design*), Pursuer, against [C.D.] (*design*), Defender, [and I required him [*or* her] to being with him [*or* her] (*specify documents*)]. This I did by (*state mode of citation*).

Date (*insert date*)   Signed

[P.Q.], Sheriff officer;
or [X.Y.], (*add designation and business address*)
Solicitor for the pursuer [*or* defender]

FORM G13   Rules 28.4(4) and 29.7(4)

Form of citation of witness or haver

CITATION

SHERIFFDOM OF (*insert name of sheriffdom*)
AT (*insert place of sheriff court*)

To [K.L.] (*design*).

You are required to attend the above sheriff court on (*insert date*) at (*insert time*) as a witness for the pursuer [*or* defender] in the action by [A.B.] (*design*), Pursuer, against [C.D.] (*design*), Defender, [and to bring with you (*specify documents*)].

(continued)

If you fail to attend without reasonable excuse, having demanded and been paid your travelling expenses, you may be ordered to pay a penalty not exceeding £250 and warrant may be granted for your arrest.

Date (*insert date*)   Signed

> [P.Q.], Sheriff officer;
> *or* [X.Y.], (*add designation and
> business address*)
> Solicitor for the pursuer [*or*
> defender]

NOTE
Claims for necessary outlays and loss of earnings within certain specified limits will be paid. Claims should be made to the person who has cited you to attend court. Proof of any loss of earnings should be given to that person.

If you wish your travelling expenses to be paid prior to your attendance you should apply for payment to the person who has cited you.

Form G14   Rules 28.4(6)(b), 28.10(4(b) and 29.16

Form of oath for witness

The witness to raise his right hand and repeat after the sheriff [*or* commissioner]: "I swear by Almighty God that I will tell the truth, the whole truth and nothing but the truth".

Form G15   Rules 28.4(6)(b), 28.10(4)(b) and 29.16

Form of affirmation for witness

The witness to repeat after the sheriff [*or* commissioner]: "I solemnly, sincerely and truly declare and affirm that I will tell the truth, the whole truth and nothing but the truth".

FORM G16 Rule 28.14(3)

Form of minute for letter of request

SHERIFFDOM OF (*insert name of sheriffdom*)
AT (*insert place of sheriff court*)

MINUTE FOR PURSUER [*or* DEFENDER]
in the cause

[A.B.] (*insert designation and address*)
Pursuer
against
[C.D.] (*insert designation and address*)
Defender

Court ref.no.

The Minuter states that the evidence specified in the attached letter of request is required for the purpose of these proceedings and craves the court to issue a letter of request to (*specify the court or tribunal having powers to obtain the evidence*) to obtain the evidence specified.

Date (*insert date*)   Signed

Solicitor for the pursuer [*or* defender *or* third party] (*add designation and business address*)

FORM G17 Rule 28.14(3)

Form of letter of request

LETTER OF REQUEST

1. Sender   (*insert name and address*)

2. Central authority of the requested state   (*insert name and address*)

3. Person to whom the executed request is to be returned   (*insert name and address*)

4. The undersigned applicant has the honour to submit the following request:

5. a. Requesting judicial authority   (*insert name and address*)
   b. The the competent authority   (*insert name of requested state*)

6. Names and addresses of the parties and their representatives
   a. Pursuer
   b. Defender
   c. Other parties

(*continued*)

169

7. Nature and purpose of the proceedings and summary of facts

8. Evidence to be obtained or other judicial act to be performed

(*Items to be completed where applicable*)

9. Identity and address of any person to be examined

10. Questions to be put to the persons to be examined or statement of the subject-matter about which they are to be examined

(*or see attached list*)

11. Documents or other property to be inspected

(*specify whether it is to be produced, copied, valued, etc.*)

12. Any requirement that the evidence be given on oath or affirmation and any special form to be used

(*in the event that the evidence cannot be taken in the manner requested, specify whether it is to be taken in such manner as provided by local law for the formal taking of evidence*)

13. Special methods or procedure to be followed

14. Request for notification of the time and place for the execution of the request and identity and address of any person to be notified

15. Request for attendance or participation of judicial personnel of the requesting authority at the execution of the letter of request

16. Specification of privilege or duty to refuse to give evidence under the law of the state of origin

17. The fees and expenses (costs) incurred will be borne by

(*insert name and address*)

(*Items to be included in all letters of request*)

18. Date of request

19. Signature and seal of the requesting authority

FORM G18   Rule 30.3(2)

Form of certificate of rate of exchange

CERTIFICATE OF RATE OF EXCHANGE

I (*insert designation and address*) certify that the rates current in London for the purchase of (*state the unit of currency in which the decree is expressed*) on (*insert date*) was (*state rate of exchange*) to the £ sterling and at this rate the sum of (*state the amount of the sum in the decree*) amounts to (*insert sterling equivalent*).

Date (*insert date*)   Signed

For and on behalf of the bank
manager or other official

Form O1   Rule 3.3(1)

Form of warrant of citation

(*Insert place and date*) Grants warrant to cite the defender (*insert name and address*) by serving upon him [*or* her] a copy of the writ and warrant on a period of notice of (*insert period of notice*) days, and ordains him [*or* her], if he [*or* she] intends to defend the action or make any claim, to lodge a notice of intention to defend with the sheriff clerk at (*insert place of sheriff court*) within the said period of notice after such service [and grants warrant to arrest on the dependence].

[Meantime grants interim interdict; *or* grants warrant to arrest to found jurisdiction; *or* sequestrates and grants warrant to inventory; *or otherwise, as the case may be.*]

Signed
Sheriff [*or* sheriff clerk]

Form O2   Rule 3.3(2)

Form of warrant of citation where time to pay direction may be applied for

(*Insert place and date*) Grants warrant to cite the defender (*insert name and address*) by serving a copy of the writ and warrant, with Form O3, on a period of notice of (*insert period of notice*) days and ordains him [*or* her] if he [*or* she] —

(a) intends to defend the action or make any claim, to lodge a notice of intention to defend; or
(b) admits the claim and intends to apply for a time to pay direction [and apply for recall or restriction of an arrestment] to lodge the appropriate part of Form O3 duly completed;

(*continued*)

with the sheriff clerk at (*insert place of sheriff court*) within the said period of notice after such service [and grants warrant to arrest on the dependence].

[Meantime grants interim interdict, *or* grants warrant to arrest to found jurisdiction; *or* sequestrates and grants warrant to inventory; *or otherwise, as the case may be.*]

Signed

Sheriff [*or* sheriff clerk]

Form O3   Rules 3.3(3), 7.3(2) and 18.5(1)(a)(i)

Form of notice to be served on defender in ordinary action where time to pay direction may be applied for

ACTION RAISED BY

PURSUER   DEFENDER

AT   SHERIFF COURT

(Including address)

COURT REF. NO.   _____   DATE OF EXPIRY OF

                  _____   PERIOD OF NOTICE

/   _____

                  _____

THIS SECTION MUST BE COMPLETED BY THE PURSUER BEFORE SERVICE

The Debtors (Scotland) Act 1987 gives you the right to apply to the court for a "time to pay direction" which is an order permitting you to pay any sum of money you are ordered to pay to the pursuer (which may include interest and court expenses) either by way of instalments or deferred lump sum. A deferred lump sum means that you must pay all the amount at one time within a period specified by the court.

When making a time to pay direction the court may recall or restrict an arrestment made on your property by the pursuer in connection with the action or debt (for example your bank account may have been frozen).

HOW TO APPLY FOR A TIME TO PAY DIRECTION WHERE YOU ADMIT THE CLAIM AND YOU DO NOT WANT TO DEFEND THE ACTION

1 Attached to this notice at pages 3 and 4 is an application for a time to pay direction, and for recall or restriction of an arrestment, if appropriate. If you want to make an application you should lodge the completed application with the sheriff clerk at the above address before the expiry of the period of notice, the date of which is given above. No court fee is payable when lodging the application.

2 Before completing the application please read carefully the notes overleaf on page 2. In the event of difficulty you may contact the court's civil department at the address above or any sheriff clerk's office, solicitor, Citizens Advice Bureau or other advice agency.

NOTE
Where this form is being served on a defender along with Form O9 (notice to additional or substitute defender) the reference to "date of expiry of period of notice" should be amended to "date for lodging of defences or an application for a time to pay direction" and the reference to "before the expiry of the period of notice" should be amended to "on or before the date for lodging of defences or an application for a time to pay direction".

HOW TO COMPLETE THE APPLICATION

PLEASE WRITE IN INK USING BLOCK CAPITALS

PART A of the application will have been completed in advance by the pursuer and gives details of the pursuer and you as the defender.
PART B – If you wish to apply to pay by instalments enter the amount and tick the appropriate box at B3(1). If you wish to apply to pay the full sum due in one deferred payment enter the period of deferment you propose at B3(2).
PART C – Give full details of your financial position in the space provided.
PART D – If you wish the court, when making the time to pay direction to recall or restrict an arrestment made in connection with the action, enter the appropriate details about what has been arrested and the place and date of the arrestment at D5, and attach the schedule of arrestment or copy.

Sign the application where indicated and detach pages 3 and 4. Retain the copy initial writ and pages 1 and 2 of this form as you may need them at a later stage. You should ensure that your application arrives at the court before the expiry of the period of notice.

WHAT WILL HAPPEN NEXT

If the pursuer objects to your application, a hearing will be fixed and the court will advise you in writing of the date and time.

If the pursuer does not object to your application, a copy of the court order for payment (called an extract decree) will be served on you by the pursuer's solicitor advising when instalment payments should commence or deferred payment be made.

(continued)

Appendix 1

APPLICATION FOR A TIME TO PAY DIRECTION
UNDER THE DEBTORS (SCOTLAND) ACT 1987

*PART A   By_____

_____

_____

DEFENDER

*(This section must be
completed by pursuer
before service)   In an action raised by

_____

_____

_____

PURSUER

PART B

1 The applicant is a defender in the action brought by the above named pursuer.
2 The defender admits the claim and applies to the court for a time to pay direction.
3 The defender applies   (1) To pay by instalments of £

(Tick one box only) EACH WEEK ☐ FORTNIGHT ☐ MONTH ☐

OR

(2) To pay the sum ordered in one payment
within   WEEKS/MONTHS

PART C

4 Defender's financial position

My   weekly fortnightly monthly My   weekly fortnightly monthly
outgoings are: ☐   ☐   ☐   income is: ☐   ☐   ☐

Rent/mortgage £   Wages/pensions £
Heating   £   Social security £
Food   £   Other   £
HP   £
Other   £
Total   £   Total   £

Dependants:
Children – how many ☐ Dependant relatives – how many ☐

Here list all capital (if any) e.g. value of house; amounts in bank or building society accounts; shares or other investments:

Here list any outstanding debts:

174

PART D

5 The defender seeks to recall or restrict an arrestment of which the details are as follows (*please state, and attach the schedule of arrestment or copy*):-

6 This application is made under sections 1(1) and 2(3) of the Debtors (Scotland) Act 1987.

Therefore the defender asks the court
> *a. to make a time to pay direction.
> *b. to recall the above arrestment.
> *c. to restrict the above arrestment (*in which case state restriction wanted*):-

*Delete what does not apply

Date (*insert date*)   Signed

                                          Defender

Form O4   Rule 5.2(1)

Form of citation

CITATION

SHERIFFDOM OF (*insert name of sheriffdom*)
AT (*insert place of sheriff court*)

[A.B.], (*insert designation and address*) Pursuer, against [C.D.], (*insert designation and address*), Defender

                                          Court ref.no.

(*Insert place and date*). You [C.D.], are hereby served with this copy writ and warrant, with Form O7 (notice of intention to defend).

Form O7 is served on you for use should you wish to intimate an intention to defend the action.

IF YOU WISH TO DEFEND THIS ACTION you should consult a solicitor with a view to lodging a notice of intention to defend (Form O7). The notice of intention to defend, together with the court fee of £ (*insert amount*) must be lodged with the sheriff clerk at the above address within 21 days (*or insert the appropriate period of notice*) of (*insert the date on which service was executed. N.B. Rule 5.3(2) relating to postal service*).

(*continued*)

IF YOU ARE UNCERTAIN WHAT ACTION TO TAKE you should consult a solicitor. You may be eligible for legal aid depending on your income, and you can get information about legal aid from a solicitor. You may also obtain advice from any Citizens Advice Bureau or other advice agency.

PLEASE NOTE THAT IF YOU DO NOTHING IN ANSWER TO THIS DOCUMENT the court may regard you as admitting the claim made against you and the pursuer may obtain decree against you in your absence.

Signed
[P.Q.], Sheriff officer,
or [X.Y.] (*add designation and business address*)
Solicitor for the pursuer

Form O5 Rule 5.2(2)

Form of citation where time to pay direction may be applied for

CITATION

SHERIFFDOM OF (*insert name of sheriffdom*)
AT (*insert place of sheriff court*)

[A.B.], (*insert designation and address*) Pursuer against [C.D.], (*insert designation and address*) Defender

Court ref.no.

(*Insert place and date*). You [C.D.], are hereby served with this copy writ and warrant, together with the following forms –
Form O3 (application for time to pay direction); and
Form O7 (notice of intention to defend).

Form O3 is served on you because it is considered that you may be entitled to apply for a time to pay direction [and for the recall or restriction of an arrestment used on the dependence of the action or in security of the debt referred to in the copy writ]. See Form O3 for further details.

IF YOU ADMIT THE CLAIM AND WISH TO APPLY FOR A TIME TO PAY DIRECTION, you must complete Form O3 and return it to the sheriff clerk at (*insert address*) within 21 days (*or insert the appropriate period of notice*) of (*insert the date on which service was executed. N.B. Rule 5.3(2) relating to postal service*).

IF YOU ADMIT THE CLAIM AND WISH TO AVOID A COURT ORDER BEING MADE AGAINST YOU, the whole sum claimed including interest and any expenses due should be paid to the pursuer or his solicitor in good time before the expiry of the period of notice.

Form O7 is served on you for use should you wish to intimate an intention to defend the action.

IF YOU WISH TO DEFEND THIS ACTION you should consult a solicitor with a view to lodging a notice of intention to defend (Form O7). The notice of intention to defend, together with the court fee of £ (*insert amount*) must be lodged with the sheriff clerk at the above address within 21 days (*or insert the appropriate period of notice*) of (*insert the date on which service was executed. N.B. Rule 5.3(2) relating to postal service*).

IF YOU ARE UNCERTAIN WHAT ACTION TO TAKE you should consult a solicitor. You may be eligible for legal aid depending on your income, and you can get information about legal aid from a solicitor. You may also obtain advice from any Citizens Advice Bureau or other advice agency.

PLEASE NOTE THAT IF YOU DO NOTHING IN ANSWER TO THIS DOCUMENT the court may regard you as admitting the claim made against you and the pursuer may obtain decree against you in your absence.

Signed
[P.Q.], Sheriff officer,
or [X.Y.] (*add designation and business address*)
Solicitor for the pursuer

Form O6   Rule 5.2(3)

Form of certificate of citation

CERTIFICATE OF CITATION

(*Insert place and date*) I,   hereby certify that upon the   day of
I duly cited [C.D.], Defender, to answer to the foregoing writ. This I did by (*state method of service; if by officer and not by post, add:* in presence of [L.M.], (*insert designation*), witness hereto with me subscribing; *and where service executed by post state whether by registered post or the first class recorded delivery service*).

(*In actions in which a time to pay direction may be applied for, state whether Form O2 and Form O3 were sent in accordance with rule 3.3*)

Signed
[P.Q.], Sheriff officer
[L.M.], witness
or [X.Y.], (*add designation and business address*)
Solicitor for the pursuer

Form O7   Rules 5.2(1) and 9.1(1)

Form of notice of intention to defend

NOTICE OF INTENTION TO DEFEND

*PART A   in an action raised at   Sheriff Court
Court Ref. No.

(*insert name and business address of solicitor for the pursuer*)	
	Pursuer

Solicitor for the pursuer   **Defender**

*(This section to be completed
by the pursuer before service)

DATE OF SERVICE: DATE OF EXPIRY OF PERIOD OF NOTICE:

---

*PART B

(*This section to be completed by the defender or the defender's solicitor and both
parts of this form returned to the sheriff clerk (*insert address of sheriff clerk*) on
or before the date of expiry of the period of notice referred to in PART A above.)

(*Insert place and date*)

[C.D.], (*insert designation and address*) Defender, intends to defend the action
raised by [A.B.], (*insert designation and address*), Pursuer, against him (and
others).

Signed
          [C.D.] Defender
          or [X.Y.] (*add designation and
          business address*)
          Solicitor for the defender

FORM O8   Rule 18.5(1)(a)(i)

**Form of notice to additional or substitute defender where time to pay direction
may be applied for**

SHERIFFDOM OF (*insert name of sheriffdom*)
AT (*insert place of sheriff court*)

To [E.F.] (*insert designation and address of additional* [or *substitute*] *defender*)
                    Court ref.no.

You [E.F.] are given notice that in this action in which [A.B.] is the pursuer and [C.D.] is the defender, your name has, by order of the court dated (*insert date of court order*) been added [*or* substituted] as a defender to the said action; and the action, originally against [C.D.] is now [*or* also] directed against you.

Enclosed with this notice are the following documents –
Copies of the [*insert as appropriate*, the pleadings as adjusted *or* closed record];
Form O3 (application for a time to pay direction); and
Form O7 (notice of intention to defend).

Form O3 is served on you because it is considered that you may be entitled to apply for a time to pay direction [and for the recall or restriction of an arrestment used on the dependence of the action or in security of the debt referred to in the copy writ]. See Form O3 for further details.

IF YOU ADMIT THE CLAIM AND WISH TO APPLY FOR A TIME TO PAY DIRECTION, you must complete Form O3 and return it to the sheriff clerk at (*insert address*) within 21 days (*or insert the appropriate period of notice*) of (*insert the date on which service was executed. N.B. Rule 5.3(2) relating to postal citation*).

IF YOU ADMIT THE CLAIM AND WISH TO AVOID A COURT ORDER BEING MADE AGAINST YOU, the whole sum claimed including interest and any expenses due should be paid to the pursuer or his solicitor in good time before the expiry of the period of notice.

Form O7 is served on you for use should you wish to intimate an intention to defend the action.

IF YOU WISH TO DEFEND THIS ACTION you should consult a solicitor with a view to lodging a notice of intention to defend (Form O7). The notice of intention to defend, together with the court fee of £ (*insert amount*) must be lodged with the sheriff clerk at the above address within 21 days (*or insert the appropriate period of notice*) of (*insert the date on which service was executed. N.B. See Rule 5.3(2) relating to postal service*).

IF YOU ARE UNCERTAIN WHAT ACTION TO TAKE you should consult a solicitor. You may be eligible for legal aid depending on your income, and you can get information about legal aid from a solicitor. You may also obtain advice from any Citizens Advice Bureau or other advice agency.

PLEASE NOTE THAT IF YOU DO NOTHING IN ANSWER TO THIS DOCUMENT the court may regard you as admitting the claim made against you and the pursuer may obtain decree against you in your absence.

Signed
[P.Q.], Sheriff officer,
or [X.Y.], (*add designation and business address*)
Solicitor for the pursuer [*or* defender]

FORM O9   Rule 18.5(1)(a)(ii)

Form of notice to additional or substitute defender

SHERIFFDOM OF (*Insert name of sheriffdom*)
AT (*insert place of sheriff court*)

To [E.F.] (*insert designation and address of additional* [or *substitute*] *defender*)
Court ref.no.

You [E.F.] are given notice that in this action in which [A.B.] is the pursuer and [C.D.] is the defender, your name has, by order of the court dated (*insert date of court order*) been added [*or* substituted] as a defender to the said action; and the action, originally against the said [C.D.] is now [*or* also] directed against you.

Enclosed with this notice are the following documents –

Copies of the [*insert as appropriate* pleadings as adjusted *or* closed record]; and Form O7 (notice of intention to defend).

Form O7 is served on you for use should you wish to intimate an intention to defend the action.

IF YOU WISH TO DEFEND THIS ACTION you should consult a solicitor with a view to lodging a notice of intention to defend (Form O7). The notice of intention to defend, together with the court fee of £ (*insert amount*) must be lodged with the sheriff clerk at the above address within 28 days (*or insert the appropriate period of notice*) of (*insert the date on which service was executed. N.B. Rule 5.3(2) relating to postal service*).

IF YOU ARE UNCERTAIN WHAT ACTION TO TAKE you should consult a solicitor. You may be eligible for legal aid depending on your income, and you can get information about legal aid from a solicitor. You may also obtain advice from any Citizens Advice Bureau or other advice agency.

PLEASE NOTE THAT IF YOU DO NOTHING IN ANSWER TO THIS DOCUMENT the court may regard you as admitting the claim made against you and the pursuer may obtain decree against you in your absence.

Signed
              [P.Q.], Sheriff officer,
              or [X.Y.] (*add designation and business address*)
              Solicitor for the pursuer [*or* defender]

Form O10

Rule 20.1

Form of third party notice

SHERIFFDOM OF (*insert name of sheriffdom*)   Court ref.no.
AT (*insert place of sheriff court*)

THIRD PARTY NOTICE
in the cause
[A.B.], (*insert designation and address*), Pursuer
against
[C.D.], (*insert designation and address*), Defender

To [E.F.]

You are given notice by [C.D.] of an order granted by Sheriff (*insert name of sheriff*) in this action in which [A.B.] is the pursuer and [C.D.] the defender. In the action the pursuer claims against the defender the sum of £   as damages in respect of (*insert brief account of the circumstances of the claim*), as more fully appears in the [*insert as appropriate*, pleadings as adjusted *or* amended *or* closed record] enclosed.

*The defender admits [*or* denies] liability to the pursuer but claims that, if he is liable to the pursuer, you are liable to relieve him [*or* her] wholly [*or* partially] of his [*or* her] liability because (*set forth contract or other right of contribution, relief, or indemnity*) as more fully appears from the defences lodged by him [*or* her] in the action.

or

*Delete
as
appro-
priate.

*The defender denies liability for the injury claimed to have been suffered by the pursuer and maintains that liability, if any, to the pursuer rests solely on you [along with (*insert names of any other person whom defender maintains is liable to him [or her] by way of contribution, relief or indemnity*)] as more fully appears from the defences lodged by him [*or* her] in the action.

or

*The defender denies liability for the injury said to have been suffered by the pursuer but maintains that if there is any liability he shares that with you, as more fully appears from the defences lodged by him [*or* her] in the action.

or

*The defender admits liability in part for the injury suffered by the pursuer but disputes the amount of damages and maintains that liability falls to be shared by you, as more fully appears from the defences lodged by him [*or* her] in the action.

or

*The defender admits liability in part for the injury suffered by the pursuer and for the damages claimed but maintains that libility falls to be shared by you, as more fully appears from the defences lodged by him [*or* her] in the action.

or

*(*Otherwise as the case may be*)

(*continued*)

IF YOU WISH TO resist either the claim of the pursuer against the defender, or the claim of the defender against you, you must lodge answers with the sheriff clerk at the above address within 28 days of (*insert the date on which service was executed, N.B. Rule 5.3(2) relating to postal service*). You must also pay the court fee of £ (*insert amount*).

Date (*insert date*)　　　　　　　　Signed

　　　　　　　　　　　　　　　　　Solicitor for the defender

FORM F1　　　　　　　　　　Rule 33.7(1)(a)

Form of intimation to children and next-of-kin an an action of divorce or separation where the defender's address is not known

Court ref.no.

To (*insert name and address as in warrant*)

You are given NOTICE that an action of divorce [*or* separation] has been raised against (*insert name*) your (*insert relationship, e.g. father, mother, brother or other relative as the case may be*). If you know of his [*or* her] present address, you are requested to inform the sheriff clerk (*insert address of sheriff clerk*) in writing immediately. If you wish to appear as a party you must lodge a minute with the sheriff clerk for leave to do so. Your minute must be lodged within 21 days of (*insert date on which intimation was given. N.B. Rule 5.3(2) relating to postal service or intimation*).

Date (*insert date*)　　　　　　　　Signed

　　　　　　　　　　　　　　　　　Solicitor for the pursuer (*add designation and business address*)

NOTE
If you decide to lodge a minute it may be in your best interest to consult a solicitor. The minute should be lodged with the sheriff clerk with the appropriate fee of (*insert amount*) and a copy of this intimation.

IF YOU ARE UNCERTAIN WHAT ACTION TO TAKE you should consult a solicitor. You may be eligible for legal aid depending on your financial circumstances, and you can get information about legal aid from a solicitor. You may also obtain advice from any Citizens Advice Bureau or other advice agency.

FORM F2   Rule 33.7(1)(b)

Form of intimation to alleged adulterer in action of divorce or separation

To (*insert name and address as in warrant*)   Court ref.no.

You are given NOTICE that in this action, you are alleged to have committed adultery. A copy of the initial writ is attached. If you wish to dispute the truth of the allegation made against you, you must lodge a minute with the sheriff clerk (*insert address of sheriff clerk*) for leave to appear as a party. Your minute must be lodged within 21 days of (*insert date on which intimation given. N.B. Rule 5.3(2) relating to postal service or intimation*).

Date (*insert date*)   Signed
                                        Solicitor for the pursuer

---

NOTE
If you decide to lodge a minute it may be in your best interest to consult a solicitor. The minute should be lodged with the sheriff clerk together with the appropriate fee of (*insert amount*) and a copy of this intimation.

IF YOU ARE UNCERTAIN WHAT ACTION TO TAKE you should consult a solicitor. You may be eligible for legal aid depending on your financial circumstances, and you can get information about legal aid from a solicitor. You may also obtain advice from any Citizens Advice Bureau or other advice agency.

FORM F3   Rule 33.7(1)(c)

Form of intimation to children, next-of-kin and *curator bonis* in an action of divorce or separation where the defender suffers from a mental disorder

To (*insert name and address as in warrant*)   Court ref.no.

You are given NOTICE that an action of divorce [*or* separation] has been raised against (*insert name, and designation*) your (*insert relationship, e.g. father, mother, brother or other relative, or ward, as the case may be*). A copy of the initial writ is enclosed. If you wish to appear as a party, you must lodge a minute with the sheriff clerk (*insert address of sheriff clerk*), for leave to do so. Your minute must be lodged within 21 days of (*insert date on which intimation was given. N.B. Rule 5.3(2) relating to postal service or intimation*).

Date (*insert date*)   Signed
                                        Solicitor for the pursuer (*insert
                                        designation and business
                                        address*)

(*continued*)

> **NOTE**
> If you decide to lodge a minute it may be in your best interest to consult a solicitor. The minute should be lodged with the sheriff clerk together with the appropriate fee of (*insert amount*) and a copy of this intimation.

> **IF YOU ARE UNCERTAIN WHAT ACTION TO TAKE** you should consult a solicitor. You may be eligible for legal aid depending on your financial circumstances, and you can get information about legal aid from a solicitor. You may also obtain advice from any Citizens Advice Bureau or other advice agency.

FORM F4 Rule 33.7(1)(d)

Form of intimation to additional spouse of either party in proceedings relating to a polygamous marriage

To (*name and address as in warrant*) Court ref.no.

You are given NOTICE that this action for divorce [*or* separation], involves (*insert name and designation*) your spouse. A copy of the initial writ is attached. If you wish to appear as a party, you must lodge a minute with the sheriff clerk (*insert address of sheriff clerk*) for leave to do so. Your minute must be lodged within 21 days of (*insert date on which intimation was given. N.B. Rule 5.3(2) relating to postal service or intimation*).

Date (*insert date*) Signed

Solicitor for the pursuer

> **NOTE**
> If you decide to lodge a minute it may be in your best interest to consult a solicitor. The minute should be lodged with the sheriff clerk with the appropriate fee of (*insert amount*) and a copy of this intimation.

> **IF YOU ARE UNCERTAIN WHAT ACTION TO TAKE** you should consult a solicitor. You may be eligible for legal aid depending on your financial circumstances, and you can get information about legal aid from a solicitor. You may also obtain advice from any Citizens Advice Bureau or other advice agency.

Appendix 1

FORM F5 Rule 33.7(1)(e)(i) and (ii)

Form of intimation to a local authority or third party who may be liable to maintain a child

To (*name and address as in warrant*)   Court ref.no.

You are given NOTICE that in this action, the court may make an order in respect of the custody of (*insert name and address*), a child in your care [*or* liable to be maintained by you]. A copy of the initial writ is attached. If you wish to appear as a party, you must lodge a minute with the sheriff clerk (*insert address of sheriff clerk*) for leave to do so. Your minute must be lodged within 21 days of (*insert date on which intimation was given. N.B. Rule 5.3(2) relating to postal service or intimation*).

Date (*insert date*)   Signed
                                     Solicitor for the pursuer

---

NOTE
The minute should be lodged with the sheriff clerk with the appropriate fee of (*insert amount*) and a copy of this intimation.

IF YOU ARE UNCERTAIN WHAT ACTION TO TAKE you should consult a solicitor. You may be eligible for legal aid depending on your financial circumstances, and you can get information about legal aid from a solicitor. You may also obtain advice from any Citizens Advice Bureau or other advice agency.

FORM F6 Rule 33.7(1)(e)(iii)

Form of intimation to person having *de facto* custody of a child

To (*name and address as in warrant*)   Court ref.no.

You are given NOTICE that in this action, the court may make an order in respect of the custody of (*insert name and address*) a child at present in your custody. A copy of the initial writ is attached. If you wish to appear as a party, you must lodge a minute with the sheriff clerk (*insert address of sheriff clerk*) for leave to do so. Your minute must be lodged within 21 days of (*insert date on which intimation was given. N.B. Rule 5.3(2) relating to postal service or intimation*).

Date (*insert date*)   Signed
                                     Solicitor for the pursuer

(*continued*)

185

Appendix 1

NOTE
If you decide to lodge a minute it may be in your best interest to consult a solicitor. The minute should be lodged with the sheriff clerk with the appropriate fee of (*insert amount*) and a copy of this intimation.

IF YOU ARE UNCERTAIN WHAT ACTION TO TAKE you should consult a solicitor. You may be entitled to legal aid depending on your financial circumstances, and you can get information about legal aid from a solicitor. You may also obtain advice from any Citizens Advice Bureau or other advice agency.

FORM F7   Rules 33.7(1)(f) and 33.19(1)(a)(i)
Form of notice to parent or guardian in action for custody of a child

1. You are given NOTICE that in this action, the pursuer seeks custody of the child (*insert name of child*). A copy of the initial writ is served on you and is attached to this notice.

2. *The pursuer, being a relative [*or* step parent] of the child, has the consent of [*or* seeks the consent of] (*insert name of parent or guardian*) who is a parent [*or* guardian] of the child, and has had care and possession of the child for three months preceding the lodging of the initial writ on (*insert date*);
OR
*The pursuer has the consent of [*or* seeks the consent of] (*insert name of parent or guardian*) who is a parent [*or* guardian] of the child and has care and possession of the child, for a period or periods before lodging the writ which amount to at least twelve months including the three months preceding the lodging of the initial writ on (*insert date*).
OR
*The pursuer has had care and possession of the child for a period before the lodging of this writ which amount to at least three years, including the three years preceding the lodging of the initial writ on (*insert date*).
OR
*The pursuer intends to establish the following as showing cause why the pursuer should be granted custody of the child (*state briefly the ground on which custody is sought or refer to the relevant article of condescendence in the writ*).

   *Delete as appropriate.

3. *If you wish to consent to the pursuer being granted custody to the child in the event of the court deciding that that was appropriate, you should complete Form F25.
OR
*(*Insert name of parent or guardian*) has consented to the pursuer being granted custody of the child in the event of the court deciding that that was appropriate.

   *Both alternative paragraphs should be struck out if the pursuer is a parent or guardian.

186

[*Insert if appropriate*   AND
The writ states that the child has been in the care and possession of the pursuer for a period or periods which amount to three years and accordingly, if that is correct, it is an offence to remove the child from the custody of the pursuer against the will of the pursuer except with the authority of the court or under the authority of any enactment or on the lawful arrest of the child.]

4. If you wish to oppose this action, and oppose the granting of custody of the child to the pursuer, you must lodge a notice of intention to defend (Form F26). See Form F26 attached for further details.

Date (*insert date*)   Signed

                                        Pursuer
                                        or Solicitor for the pursuer (*add designation and business address*)

NOTE
IF YOU ARE UNCERTAIN WHAT ACTION TO TAKE you should consult a solicitor. You may be entitled to legal aid depending on your financial circumstances, and you can get information about legal aid from a solicitor. You may also obtain advice from any Citizens Advice Bureau or other advice agency.

FORM F8   Rules 33.7(1)(g), 33.7(4) and 33.12(2)

Form of notice to local authority under section 49(1) of the Children Act 1975

                                        Court ref.no.
To (*insert name and address*)

You are given NOTICE that the pursuer has presented an initial writ to the sheriff court at (*insert address*) for the custody of the child (*insert name of child*). A copy of the initial writ is enclosed.

2. You are required under section 49(2) of the Children Act 1975 to submit to the court a report on all the circumstances of the child and on the proposed arrangements for the care and upbringing of the child.

Date (*insert date*)   Signed

                                        Solicitor for the pursuer (*add designation and business address*)

(*continued*)

187

FORM F9   Rule 33.7(1)(h)

Form of intimation in an action which affects a child

To (*insert name and address as in warrant*)   Court ref.no.

You are given NOTICE that in this action, the pursuer craves the court to (*insert details of the crave(s) that affect the child*) which affect you. A copy of the initial writ is attached. If you wish to apply to appear as a party, you must lodge a minute with the sheriff clerk (*insert address of sheriff clerk*) for leave to do so. Your minute must be lodged within 21 days of (*insert date on which intimation was given. N.B. Rule 5.3(2) relating to postal service or intimation*).

Date (*insert date*)   Signed
                               Solicitor for the pursuer

NOTE
If you decide to lodge a minute it may be in your best interest to consult a solicitor. The minute should be lodged with the sheriff clerk with the appropriate fee of (*insert amount*) and a copy of this intimation.

IF YOU ARE UNCERTAIN WHAT ACTION TO TAKE you should consult a solicitor. You may be eligible for legal aid depending on your financial circumstances, and you can get information about legal aid from a solicitor. You may also obtain advice from any Citizens Advice Bureau or other advice agency.

FORM F10   Rule 33.7(1)(i)

Form of intimation to creditor in application for order for the transfer of property under section 8 of the Family Law (Scotland) Act 1985

To (*insert name and address as in warrant*)   Court ref.no.

You are given NOTICE that in this action an order is sought for the transfer of property (*specify the order*), over which you hold a security. A copy of the initial writ is attached. If you wish to appear as a party, you must lodge a minute with the sheriff clerk (*insert address of sheriff clerk*) for leave to do so. Your minute must be lodged within 21 days of (*insert date on which intimation was given. N.B. Rule 5.3(2) relating to postal service or intimation*).

Date (*insert date*)   Signed
                               Solicitor for the pursuer

NOTE
If you decide to lodge a minute it may be in your best interest to consult a solicitor. The minute should be lodged with the sheriff clerk with the appropriate fee of (*insert amount*) and a copy of this intimation.

IF YOU ARE UNCERTAIN WHAT ACTION TO TAKE you should consult a solicitor. You may be eligible for legal aid depending on your financial circumstances, and you can get information about legal aid from a solicitor. You may also obtain advice from any Citizens Advice Bureau or other advice agency.

FORM F11   Rule 33.7(1)(j)

Form of intimation in an action where the pursuer makes an application for an order under section 18 of the Family Law (Scotland) Act 1985

To (*insert name and address as in warrant*)   Court ref.no.

You are given NOTICE that in this action, the pursuer craves the court to make an order under section 18 of the Family Law (Scotland) Act 1985. A copy of the initial writ is attached. If you wish to apply to appear as a party, you must lodge a minute with the sheriff clerk (*insert address of sheriff clerk*) for leave to do so. Your minute must be lodged within 21 days of (*insert date on which intimation was given. N.B. Rule 5.3(2) relating to postal service or intimation*).

Date (*insert date*)   Signed
                                        Solicitor for the pursuer

---

NOTE
If you decide to lodge a minute it may be in your best interest to consult a solicitor. The minute should be lodged with the sheriff clerk with the appropriate fee of (*insert amount*) and a copy of this intimation.

IF YOU ARE UNCERTAIN WHAT ACTION TO TAKE you should consult a solicitor. You may be eligible for legal aid depending on your financial circumstances, and you can get information about legal aid from a solicitor. You may also obtain advice from any Citizens Advice Bureau or other advice agency.

FORM F12   Rule 33.7(1)(k)

Form of intimation in an action where a non-entitled pursuer makes an application for an order under the Matrimonial Homes (Family Protection) (Scotland) Act 1981

To (*insert name and address as in warrant*)   Court ref.no.

You are given NOTICE that in this action, the pursuer craves the court to make an order under section of (*insert the section under which the order(s) sought*) of the Matrimonial Homes (Family Protection) (Scotland) Act 1981. A copy of the initial writ is attached. If you wish to apply to appear as a party, you must lodge a minute with the sheriff clerk (*insert address of sheriff clerk*) for leave to do so. Your minute must be lodged within 21 days of (*insert date on which intimation was given. N.B. Rule 5.3 (2) relating to postal service or intimation*).

Date (*insert date*)   Signed
                                  Solicitor for the pursuer

NOTE
If you decide to lodge a minute it may be in your best interest to consult a solicitor. The minute should be lodged with the sheriff clerk with the appropriate fee of (*insert amount*) and a copy of this intimation.

IF YOU ARE UNCERTAIN WHAT ACTION TO TAKE you should consult a solicitor. You may be eligible for legal aid depending on your financial circumstances, and you can get information about legal aid from a solicitor. You may also obtain advice from any Citizens Advice Bureau or other advice agency.

FORM F13   Rule 33.8(3)

Form of intimation to person with whom an improper association is alleged to have occurred

To (*insert name and address as in warrant*)   Court ref.no.

You are given NOTICE that in this action, the defender is alleged to have had an improper association with you. A copy of the initial writ is attached. If you wish to dispute the truth of the allegation made against you, you must lodge a minute with the sheriff clerk (*insert address of sheriff clerk*) for leave to appear as party. Your minute must be lodged within 21 days of (*insert date on which intimation was given. N.B. Rule 5.3(2) relating to postal service or intimation*).

Date (*insert date*)   Signed
                                  Solicitor for the pursuer

NOTE
If you decide to lodge a minute it may be in your best interest to consult a solicitor. The minute should be lodged with the sheriff clerk with the appropriate fee of (*insert amount*) and a copy of this intimation.

IF YOU ARE UNCERTAIN WHAT ACTION TO TAKE you should consult a solicitor. You may be eligible for legal aid depending on your financial circumstances, and you can get information about legal aid from a solicitor. You may also obtain advice from any Citizens Advice Bureau or other advice agency.

FORM F14   Rule 33.10

Form of warrant of citation in family action

(*Insert place and date*)
Grants warrant to cite the defender (*insert name and address of defender*) by serving upon him [*or* her] a copy of the writ and warrant upon a period of notice of (*insert period of notice*) days, and ordains the defender to lodge a notice of intention to defend with the sheriff clerk at (*insert address of sheriff court*) if he [*or* she] wishes to:
  (a) challenge the jurisdiction of the court;
  (b) oppose any claim made or order sought;
  (c) make any claim or seek any order.

[Meantime grants interim interdict, *or* warrant to arrest on the dependence].

FORM F15   Rules 33.11(1) and 33.13(1)(a)

Form of citation in family action

CITATION

SHERIFFDOM OF (*insert name of sheriffdom*)
AT (*insert place of sheriff court*)

[A.B.], (*insert designation and address*) Pursuer, against [C.D.], (*insert designation and address*), Defender.
                                Court ref.no.

(*Insert place and date*) You [C.D.], are hereby served with this copy writ and warrant, with Form F26 (notice of intention to defend) [and (*insert details of any other form of notice served, e.g. any of the forms served in accordance with rule 33.14*)].

(*continued*)

Form F26 is served on you for use should you wish to intimate an intention to defend the action.

IF YOU WISH TO –
(a) challenge the jurisdiction of the court;
(b) oppose any claim made or order sought;
(c) make any claim or seek any order; or
(d) seek any order;
you should consult a solicitor with a view to lodging a notice of intention to defend (Form F26). The notice of intention to defend, together with the court fee of £ (*insert amount*) must be lodged with the sheriff clerk at the above address within 21 days (*or insert appropriate period of notice*) of (*insert the date on which service was executed. N.B. Rule 5.3(2) relating to postal service or intimation*).

IF YOU ARE UNCERTAIN WHAT ACTION TO TAKE you should consult a solicitor. You may be entitled to legal aid depending on your financial circumstances, and you can get information about legal aid from a solicitor. You may also obtain advice from any Citizens Advice Bureau or other advice agency.

PLEASE NOTE THAT IF YOU DO NOTHING IN ANSWER TO THIS DOCUMENT the court may regard you as admitting the claim made against you and the pursuer may obtain decree against you in your absence.

Signed
[P.Q.], Sheriff officer
or
[X.Y.] (*add designation and business address*)
Solicitor for the pursuer

FORM F16   Rule 33.11(2)

Form of certificate of citation in family action

CERTIFICATE OF CITATION

(*Insert place and date*) I,   hereby certify that upon the   day of
I duly cited [C.D.], Defender, to answer to the foregoing writ. This I did by (*state
method of service; if by officer and not by post, add:* in presence of [L.M.], (*insert
designation*), witness hereto with me subscribing); *and* (*insert details of any forms
of intimation or notice sent including details of the person to whom intimation
sent and the method of service*).

Signed
                    [P.W.], Sheriff officer
                    [L.M.], witness
                    or
                    [X.Y.], (*add designation and
                    business address*)
                    Solicitor for the pursuer

FORM F17   Rule 33.13(1)(c)

Form of request to medical officer of hospital or similar institution

To (*insert name and address of medical officer*)
In terms of rule 33.13(1)(c) of the Ordinary Cause Rules of the Sheriff Court a
copy of the initial writ at the instance of (*insert name and address of pursuer*),
Pursuer, against (*insert name and address of defender*), Defender, is enclosed and
you are requested to
(a) deliver it personally to (*insert name of defender*), and
(b) explain the contents to him or her,
unless you are satisfied that such delivery or explanation would be dangerous to
his or her health or mental condition. You are further requested to complete and
return to me in the enclosed stamped addressed envelope the certificate appended
hereto, making necessary deletions.

Date (*insert date*)   Signed
                                        Solicitor for the pursuer (*add
                                        designation and business
                                        address*)

FORM F18   Rules 33.13(1)(d) and 33.13(2)

Form of certificate by medical officer of hospital or similar institution

Court ref.no.

I (*insert name and designation*) certify that I have received a copy initial writ in an action of (*type of family action to be inserted by the party requesting service*) at the instance of (*insert name and designation*), Pursuer, against (*insert name and designation*), Defender, and that

*I have on the   day of   personally delivered a copy thereof to the said defender who is under my care at (*insert address*) and I have explained the contents or purport thereof to him or her, *or*

*I have not delivered a copy thereof to the said defender who is under my care at (*insert address*) and I have not explained the contents or purport thereof to him or her because (*state reasons*).

Date (*insert date*)   Signed

                              Medical officer (*add
                              designation and address*)

*Delete as appropriate.

FORM F19   Rule 33.14(1)(a)(i)

Form of notice to defender where it is stated that defender consents to the granting of decree of divorce

You are given NOTICE that the copy initial writ served on you with this notice states that you consent to the grant of decree of divorce.

1. If you do so consent the consequences for you are that –
   (a) provided the pursuer establishes the fact that he [*or* she] has not cohabited with you at any time during a continuous period of two years after the date of your marriage and immediately preceding the bringing of this action and that you consent, a decree of divorce will be granted;
   (b) on the grant of a decree of divorce you may lose your rights of succession to the pursuer's estate; and
   (c) decree of divorce will end the marriage thereby affecting any right to such pension as may depend on the marriage continuing, or, on your being left a widow the state widow's pension will not be payable to you when the pursuer dies.
Apart from these, there may be other consequences for you depending upon your particular circumstances.

2. You are entitled, whether or not you consent to the grant of decree to apply to the sheriff in this action −
   (a) to make financial or other provision for you under the Family Law (Scotland) Act 1985;
   (b) for an order under the Law Reform (Parent and Child) (Scotland) Act 1986 relating to parental rights (including custody and access) to any child of the marriage, or any child accepted as such, who is under 16 years of age; or
   (c) for any other competent order.

3. **IF YOU WISH TO APPLY FOR ANY OF THE ABOVE ORDERS** you should consult a solicitor with a view to lodging a notice of intention to defend (Form 26).

4. If, after consideration, you wish to consent to decree, you should complete and sign the attached form of notice of consent (Form F20) and send it to the sheriff clerk at the sheriff court referred to in the initial writ within 21 days of (*insert the date on which service was executed. N.B. Rule 5.3(2) relating to postal service*).

5. If at a later stage you wish to withdraw your consent you must inform the sheriff clerk immediately in writing that you withdraw your consent to decree being granted against you in this action.

Date (*insert date*) Signed

Solicitor for the pursuer (*add designation and business address*)

FORM F20   Rule 33.14(1)(a)(i) and 33.18(1)

Court ref.no.

Form of notice of consent in actions of divorce under section 1(2)(d) of the Divorce (Scotland) Act 1976

[A.B.], (*insert designation and address*), Pursuer, against [C.D.], (*insert designation and address*), Defender

I (*full name and address of the defender to be inserted by pursuer or pursuer's solicitor before sending notice*) have received a copy of the initial writ in the action against me at the instance of (*full name and address of pursuer to be inserted by pursuer or pursuer's solicitor before sending notice*). I understand that it states that I consent to the grant of decree of divorce in this action. I have considered the consequences for me mentioned in the notice (Form F19) sent to me with this notice. I consent to the grant of decree of divorce in this action.

Date (*insert date*)   Signed
                       Defender

FORM F21   Rule 33.14(1)(a)(ii)

Form of notice to defender where it is stated that defender consents to the granting of decree of separation

You are given NOTICE that the copy initial writ served on you with this notice states that you consent to the grant of decree of separation.

1. If you do so consent the consequences for you are that –
   (a) provided the pursuer establishes the fact that he [*or* she] has not cohabited with you at any time during a continuous period of two years after the date of your marriage and imediately preceding the bringing of this action and that you consent, a decree of separation will be granted;
   (b) on the grant of decree of separation you will be obliged to live apart from the pursuer but the marriage will continue to subsist; you will continue to have a legal obligation to support your wife [*or* husband] and children;
Apart from these, there may be other consequences for you depending upon your particular circumstances.

2. If you do consent to the grant of decree you may apply to the sheriff in this action –
   (a) to make financial or other provision for you under the Family Law (Scotland) Act 1985;
   (b) for an order under the Law Reform (Parent and Child) (Scotland) Act 1986 relating to parental rights (including custody and access) to any child of the marriage, or any child accepted as such, who is under 16 years of age; or
   (c) for any other competent order.

3. **IF YOU WISH TO APPLY FOR ANY OF THE ABOVE ORDERS** you should consult a solicitor with a view to lodging a notice of intention to defend (Form F26).

4. If after consideration, you wish to consent to decree, you should complete and sign the attached Form of notice of consent (Form F22) and send it to the sheriff clerk at the sheriff court referred to in the initial writ and other papers within 21 days of (*insert the date on which service was executed. N.B. Rule 5.3(2) relating to postal service or intimation*).

5. If at a later stage you wish to withdraw your consent you must inform the sheriff clerk immediately in writing that you withdraw your consent to decree being granted against you in this action.

Date (*insert date*)   Signed

                                     Solicitor for the pursuer
                                     (*add designation and
                                     business address*)

FORM F22   Rules 33.14(1)(a)(ii) and 33.18(1)

Form of notice of consent in actions of separation under section 1(2)(d) of the Divorce (Scotland) Act 1976

Court ref.no.

[A.B.], (*insert designation and address*), Pursuer against [C.D.], (*insert designation and address*), Defender

I (*full name and address of the defender to be inserted by pursuer or pursuer's solicitor before sending notice*) confirm that I have received a copy of the initial writ in the action against me at the instance of (*full name and address of pursuer to be inserted by pursuer or pursuer's solicitor before sending notice*). I understand that it states that I consent to the grant of decree of separation in this action. I have considered the consequences for me mentioned in the notice (Form F21) sent together with this notice. I consent to the grant of decree of separation in this action.

Date (*insert date*)   Signed
                             Defender

FORM F23   Rule 33.14(1)(b)(i)

Form of notice to defender in an action of divorce where it is stated there has been five years' non-cohabitation

You are given NOTICE that –

1. The copy initial writ served on you with this notice states that there has been no cohabitation between you and the pursuer at any time during a continuous period of five years after the date of the marriage and immediately preceding the commencement of this action. If the pursuer establishes this as a fact and the sheriff is satisfied that the marriage has broken down irretrievably, a decree will be granted, unless the sheriff is of the opinion that to grant decree would result in grave financial hardship to you.

2. Decree of divorce will end the marriage thereby affecting any right to such pension as may depend on the marriage continuing, or, on your being left a widow the state widow's pension will not be payable to you when the pursuer dies. You may also lose your rights of succession to the pursuer's estate.

3. You are entitled, whether or not you dispute that there has been no such cohabitation during that five year period, to apply to the sheriff in this action –
   (a) to make financial or other provision for you under the Family Law (Scotland) Act 1985;
   (b) for an order under the Law Reform (Parent and Child) (Scotland) Act 1986 relating to parental rights (including custody and access) to any child of the marriage, or any child accepted as such, who is under 16 years of age; or
   (c) for any other competent order.

(continued)

4. IF YOU WISH TO APPLY FOR ANY OF THE ABOVE ORDERS you should consult a solicitor with a view to lodging a notice of intention to defend (Form F26).

Date (*insert date*)   Signed

Solicitor for the pursuer (*add designation and business address*)

FORM F24   Rule 33.14(1)(b)(ii)

Form of notice to defender in an action of separation where it is stated there has been five years' non-cohabitation

You are given NOTICE that –

1. The copy initial writ served on you together with this notice states that there has been no cohabitation between you and the pursuer at any time during a continuous period of five years after the date of the marriage and immediately preceding the commencement of this action and that if the pursuer establishes this as a fact, and the sheriff is satisfied that there are grounds justifying decree of separation, a decree will be granted, unless the sheriff is of the opinion that to grant decree would result in grave financial hardship to you.

2. On the granting of decree of separation you will be obliged to live apart from the pursuer but the marriage will continue to subsist. You will continue to have a legal obligation to support your wife [*or* husband] and children.

3. You are entitled, whether or not you dispute that there has been no such cohabitation during that five year period, to apply to the sheriff in this action –
   (a) to make provision under the Family Law (Scotland) Act 1985;
   (b) for an order under the Law Reform (Parent and Child) (Scotland) Act 1986 relating to parental rights (including custody and access) to any child of the marriage, or any child accepted as such, who is under 16 years of age; or
   (c) for any other competent order.

4. IF YOU WISH TO APPLY FOR ANY OF THE ABOVE ORDERS you should consult a solicitor with a view to lodging a notice of intention to defend (Form F26).

Date (*insert date*)   Signed

Solicitor for the pursuer (*add designation and business address*)

FORM F25 Rules 33.19(1)(a)(ii) and 33.19(2)(i)

**Form of consent of parent or guardian in proceedings for custody of children
under section 47 of the Children Act 1975**

Court ref.no.

[A.B.], (*insert designation and address*), Pursuer, against [C.D.], (*insert designation and address*), Defender

I, (*insert name and address*) confirm that I am the mother [*or* father *or* guardian] of the child (*insert full name of the child as given on birth certificate, and the child's present address*). I understand that if I consent to the granting of custody to the pursuer, the care, possession and control of the child may be granted to the pursuer by the court. I hereby consent to the making of a custody order in relation to the child (*insert name of child*) in favour of (*insert name and address of pursuer*).

Dated at (*insert place*) on the   day of   19 .

Signature of person consenting . . . .

Signature of Witness . . . .   Signature of Witness . . . .
*Full Name . . . .   *Full Name . . . .
*Designation . . . .   *Designation . . . .
*Address . . . .   *Address . . . .
. . . .

*Please complete in block capitals

FORM F26   Rules 33.11(1) and 33.34(2)

Form of notice of intention to defend in a family action

NOTICE OF INTENTION TO DEFEND

*PART A
Court ref.no.

(Insert name and business address of solicitor for the pursuer)	In an action raised at Sheriff Court

Solicitor for the pursuer

Pursuer

Defender

*(This section to be completed
by the pursuer before service)

DATE OF SERVICE: DATE OF EXPIRY OF PERIOD OF NOTICE:

---

*PART B

*(This section to be completed by the defender or defender's solicitor, and both
parts of the form returned to the sheriff clerk at the above sheriff court on or before
the date of expiry of the period of notice referred to in PART A above.)

(Insert place and date)

[C.D.] *(insert designation and address)*, Defender, intends to
    (a) challenge the jurisdiction of the court;
    (b) oppose a crave in the initial writ;
    (c) make a claim;
    (d) seek an order;
in the action against him or her raised by [A.B.], *(insert designation and address)*,
Pursuer, against him [*or* her].

Signed
    [C.D.], Defender
    or [X.Y.], *(add designation and
    business address)*
    Solicitor for the defender

Appendix 1

FORM F27   Rule 33.29(1)(b)

Form of minute for decree in family action to which rule 33.28 applies

(*Insert name of solicitor for the pursuer*) having considered the evidence contained in the affidavits and the other documents all as specified in the schedule hereto, and being satisfied that upon the evidence a motion for decree (in terms of the crave of the initial writ) [*or in such restricted terms as may be appropriate*] may properly be made, moves the court accordingly.

In respect whereof
Signed
                    Solicitor for the pursuer (*add
                    designation and business
                    address*)

SCHEDULE
(*Number and specify documents considered*)

FORM F28   Rules 33.40(c) and 33.64(1)(c)

Form of notice of intimation to local authority or third party to whom care of a child is to be given

To (*name and address as in warrant*)   Court ref.no.

You are given NOTICE that in this action, the sheriff proposes to commit to your care the child (*insert name and address*). A copy of the initial writ is attached. If you wish to appear as a party, you must lodge a minute with the sheriff clerk (*insert address of sheriff clerk*) for leave to do so. Your minute must be lodged within 21 days of (*insert date on which intimation was given. N.B. Rule 5.3(2) relating to postal service or intimation*).

Date (*insert date*)   Signed
                    Solicitor for the pursuer

NOTE
If you decide to lodge a minute it may be in your best interest to consult a solicitor. The minute should be lodged with the sheriff clerk with the appropriate fee of (*insert amount*) and a copy of this intimation.

IF YOU ARE UNCERTAIN WHAT ACTION TO TAKE you should consult a solicitor. You may be entitled to legal aid depending on your financial circumstances, and you can get information about legal aid from a solicitor. You may also obtain advice from any Citizens Advice Bureau or other advice agency.

Appendix 1

FORM F29   Rules 33.41 and 33.64(2)

Form of notice of intimation to local authority of supervision order

[A.B.], (*insert designation and address*), Pursuer, against [C.D.], (*insert designation and address*), Defender

To (*insert name and address of local authority*)   Court ref. no.

You are given NOTICE that on (*insert date*) in the Sheriff Court at (*insert place*) the sheriff made a supervision order under section 12 of the Matrimonial Proceedings (Children) Act 1958 [*or* section 11(1)(b) of the Guardianship Act 1973] placing the child (*insert name and address of child*) under your supervision. A certified copy of the sheriff's interlocutor is attached.

Date (*insert date*)   Signed

                                        Sheriff clerk (depute)

FORM F30   Rules 33.72(1) and 33.72(2)

Form of certificate of delivery of documents to chief constable

(*Insert place and date*) I,   hereby certify that upon the   day of
I duly delivered to (*insert name and address*) chief constable of (*insert name of constabulary*) (*insert details of the documents delivered*). This I did by (*state method of service*).

                          Signed
                          Solicitor for the pursuer (*add
                          designation and business
                          address*)

FORM F31   Rule 33.74(1)

Form of simplified divorce application under section 1(2)(d) of the Divorce (Scotland) Act 1976

Sheriff Clerk
Sheriff Court House
....
....
....
(Telephone) ....

APPLICATION FOR DIVORCE WITH CONSENT OF OTHER PARTY TO THE MARRIAGE (HUSBAND AND WIFE HAVING LIVED APART FOR AT LEAST TWO YEARS)

Before completing this form, you should have read the leaflet entitled "Do it

202

yourself Divorce", which explains the circumstances in which a divorce may be sought by this method. If simplified procedure appears to suit your circumstances, you may use this form to apply for divorce. Below you will find directions designed to assist you with your application. Please follow them carefully. In the event of difficulty, you may contact any sheriff clerk's office or Citizens Advice Bureau.

Directions for making application

WRITE IN INK, USING BLOCK CAPITALS

Application (Part 1)	1. Complete and sign Part 1 of the form (pages 3–7), paying particular attention to the notes opposite each section.
Consent of husband/wife (Part 2)	2. When you have completed Part 1 of the form, attach the (blue) instruction sheet SP3 to it and send both documents to your spouse for completion of the consent at Part 2 (page 9).

NOTE: If your spouse does NOT complete and sign the form of consent, your application cannot proceed further under the simplified procedure. In that event, if you still wish to obtain a divorce, you should consult a solicitor.

Affidavit (Part 3)	3. When the application has been returned to you with the consent (Part 2) duly completed and signed, you should take the form to a Justice of the Peace, Notary Public, Commissioner for Oaths or other duly authorised person so that your affidavit at Part 3 (page 10) may be completed and sworn.
Returning completed application form to court	4. When directions 1–3 above have been complied with, your application is now ready to be sent to the sheriff clerk at the above address. With it you must enclose:

(i) your marriage certificate (the document headed "Extract of an entry in a Register of Marriages", which will be returned to you in due course), and
(ii) either a cheque or postal order in respect of the court fee, crossed and made payable to "the Sheriff Clerk".
or a completed form SP15, claiming exemption from the court fee.
5. Receipt of your application will be promptly acknowledged. Should you wish to withdraw the application for any reason, please contact the sheriff clerk immediately.

(continued)

Appendix 1

PART 1

WRITE IN INK, USING BLOCK CAPITALS

1. NAME AND ADDRESS OF APPLICANT

Surname . . . .
Other name(s) in full . . . .
. . . .

Present address . . . .
. . . .
Daytime telephone number (if any) . . . .

2. NAME AND ADDRESS OF SPOUSE

Surname . . . .
Other name(s) in full . . . .
. . . .
Present address . . . .
. . . .
. . . .
Daytime telephone number (if any) . . . .

3. JURISDICTION

Please indicate with a tick ( ) in the appropriate box or boxes which of the following apply:

PART A

(i) I consider myself to be domiciled in Scotland

(ii) I have lived in Scotland for a period of at least 12 months immediately before the date of signing this application

(iii) My spouse considers himself or herself to be domiciled in Scotland

(iv) My spouse has lived in Scotland for a period of at least 12 months immediately before the date of signing this application

PART B

(v) I have lived at the address shown in paragraph 1 above for at least 40 days immediately before the date I signed this application

(vi)   My spouse has lived at the address shown in paragraph 2 above
        for at least 40 days immediately before the date I signed this
        application

4. DETAILS OF PRESENT MARRIAGE

Place of Marriage . . . .(Registration District)

Date of Marriage: Day . . . . .month . . . . .year . . . .

5. PERIOD OF SEPARATION

(i)   Please state the date on which you ceased to live with your
        spouse. (If more than 2 years, just give the month and
        year) Day . . . . . Month . . . . . Year . . . . .

(ii)   Have you lived with your spouse since that date?   *[YES/NO]

(iii)   If yes, for how long in total did you live together before
        finally separating again?
                            . . . . .months

6. RECONCILIATION

Is there any reasonable prospect of reconciliation with your
spouse?   *[YES/NO]

Do you consider that the marriage has broken down
irretrievably?   *[YES/NO]

7. CONSENT

Does your spouse consent to a divorce being granted?   *[YES/NO]

8. MENTAL DISORDER

Is your spouse suffering from any mental disorder (whether
illness or handicap?)   *[YES/NO]

9. CHILDREN

Are there any children of the marriage under the age of 16?   *[YES/NO]

(continued)

10. OTHER COURT ACTIONS

Are you aware of any court actions currently proceeding in any
country (including Scotland) which may affect your marriage?

(If yes, give details)   *[YES/NO]

*Delete as
appropriate

11. REQUEST FOR DIVORCE AND DISCLAIMER OF FINANCIAL PROVISION

I confirm that the facts stated in paragraphs 1 – 10 above apply to my marriage.

I do NOT ask the sheriff to make any financial provision in connection with this
application.

I request the sheriff to grant decree of divorce from my spouse.

Date   Signature of applicant ....

IMPORTANT

Part 1 MUST be completed, signed and dated before sending the application form
to your spouse.

CONSENT BY APPLICANT'S SPOUSE TO DIVORCE

NOTE: Before completing this part of the form, please
read the notes opposite (page 8)

I, ...
(*Insert full name, in BLOCK letters, of Applicant's
spouse*)

residing at

....
(*Insert address, also in BLOCK letters*)
....
....

HEREBY STATE THAT

(a)   I have read Part 1 of this application;
(b)   the Applicant has lived apart from me for a continuous period of two
       years immediately preceding the date of the application (paragraph 11 of
       Part 1);
(c)   I do not ask the sheriff to make any financial provision for me including –
       (i) the payment by the Applicant of a periodical allowance (i.e. a regular
           payment of money weekly or monthly, etc. for maintenance);

(ii) the payment by the Applicant of a capital sum (i.e. a lump sum payment);
(d)   I understand that divorce may result in the loss to me of property rights; and
(e)   I CONSENT TO DECREE OF DIVORCE BEING GRANTED IN RESPECT OF THIS APPLICATION.

Date   Signature of applicant ....

NOTE: You may withdraw your consent, even after giving it, at any time before divorce is granted by the sheriff. Should you wish to do so, please contact the sheriff clerk immediately.

PART 3

APPLICANT'S AFFIDAVIT

To be completed by the Applicant only after Parts 1 and 2 have been signed and dated.
I, (*insert Applicant's full name*) ....
residing at (*insert Applicant's present home address*) ....
....
....

SWEAR that to the best of my knowledge and belief:

(1) the facts stated in Part 1 of this Application are true; and

(2) the signature in Part 2 of this Application is that of my *husband/wife.

Signature of Applicant ....

To be completed   SWORN at (*insert place*)...........................
by Justice of the   this ....day of ....19 ....
Peace, Notary Public   before me (*insert full name*) ....
or Commissioner for   (*insert full address*)...............................
Oaths   ....
                       ....
                       Signature ....

                       *Justice of the Peace/Notary Public/Commissioner for Oaths

                       *Delete as appropriate

Appendix 1

FORM F32   Rule 33.74(1)(b)

**Form of consent to simplified divorce application under section 1(2)(d)
of the Divorce (Scotland) Act 1976**

(*Insert name and address of consenting spouse*)

CONSENT TO APPLICATION FOR DIVORCE (HUSBAND AND WIFE
HAVING LIVED APART FOR AT LEAST TWO YEARS)

In Part 1 of the enclosed application form your spouse is applying for divorce
on the ground that the marriage has broken down irretrievably because you
and he [*or* she] have lived apart for at least two years and you consent to the
divorce being granted.

Such consent must be given formally in writing at Part 2 of the application
form. BEFORE completing that part, you are requested to read it over
carefully so that you understand the effects of consenting to divorce.
Thereafter if you wish to consent –

(a)   check the details given by the Applicant at Part 1 of the form to ensure
        that they are correct to the best of your knowledge;
(b)   complete Part 2 (Consent by Applicant's spouse to divorce) by entering
        your name and address at the appropriate place and adding your
        signature and the date; and
(c)   return the whole application form to your spouse at the address given in
        Part 1.

Once your husband or wife has completed the remainder of the form and has
submitted it to the court, a copy of the whole application (including your
consent) will later be served upon you formally by the sheriff clerk.

In the event of the divorce being granted, you will automatically be sent a copy
of the extract decree. (Should you change your address before receiving the
copy extract decree, please notify the sheriff clerk immediately.)

If you do NOT wish to consent please return the application form, with Part 2
uncompleted, to your spouse and advise him or her of your decision.
        The sheriff will NOT grant a divorce under this application if part of the form
is not completed by you.

Sheriff clerk (depute)
Sheriff Court (*insert address*)

FORM F33   Rule 33.74(2)

Form of simplified divorce application under section 1(2)(e) of the Divorce (Scotland) Act 1976

Sheriff Clerk
Sheriff Court House
....
....
(Telephone) ....

APPLICATION FOR DIVORCE (HUSBAND AND WIFE HAVING LIVED APART FOR AT LEAST FIVE YEARS)
Before completing this form, you should have read the leaflet entitled "Do it yourself Divorce", which explains the circumstances in which a divorce may be sought by this method. If the simplified procedure appears to suit your circumstances, you may use this form to apply for divorce.
Below you will find directions designed to assist you with your application. Please follow them carefully. In the event of difficulty, you may contact any sheriff clerk's office or Citizens Advice Bureau.

Directions for making application

WRITE IN INK USING BLOCK CAPITALS

Application   1. Complete and sign Part 1 of the form (pages 3 – 7), paying
(Part 1)   particular attention to the notes opposite each section.

Affidavits   2. When you have completed Part 1, you should take the forrm
(Part 2)   to a Justice of the Peace, Notary Public, Commissioner for
                   Oaths or other duly authorised person in order that your
                   affidavit in Part 2 (page 8) may be completed and sworn.

Returning   3. When directions 1 and 2 above have been complied with, your
completed   application is now ready to be sent to the sheriff clerk at the
application   above address. With it you must enclose:
form to court   (i) your marriage certificate (the document headed "Extract
                   of an entry in a Register of Marriages", which will be returned
                   to you in due course). Check the notes on page 2 to see if you
                   need to obtain a letter from the General Register Office
                   stating that there is no record of your spouse having divorced
                   you, and
                       (ii) either a cheque or postal order in respect of the court fee,
                   crossed and made out to the "the Sheriff Clerk".

4. Receipt of your application will be promptly acknowledged. Should you wish to withdraw the application for any reason, please contact the sheriff clerk immediately.

(continued)

Appendix 1

PART 1

WRITE IN INK, USING BLOCK CAPITALS

1. NAME AND ADDRESS OF APPLICANT

Surname ....

Other name(s) in full...........................

Present address ....

....

....

Daytime telephone number (if any) ....

2. NAME OF SPOUSE

Surname ....
Other name(s) in full...........................

3. ADDRESS OF SPOUSE (if the address of your spouse is not known, please enter 'not known' in this paragraph and proceed to paragraph 4)

Present address ....

....

....

Daytime telephone number (if any) ....

4. Only complete this paragraph if you do not know the present address of your spouse

NEXT-OF-KIN

Name...
Address..

....

....

Relationship
to your spouse ....

5. CHILDREN OF THE MARRIAGE

Names and dates of birth   Addresses
....
....
....
....
....

If insufficient space is available to list all the children of the marriage, please continue on a separate sheet and attach to this form.

6. JURISDICTION Please indicate with a tick ( ) in the appropriate box or boxes which of the following apply:

PART A

(i)   I consider myself to be domiciled in Scotland

(ii)   I have lived in Scotland for a period of at least 12 months immediately before the date of signing this application

(iii) My spouse considers himself or herself to be domiciled in Scotland

(iv)   My spouse has lived in Scotland for a period of at least 12 months immediately before the date of signing this application

PART B

(v)   I have lived at the address shown in paragraph 1 above for at least 40 days immediately before the date I signed this application

(vi)   My spouse has lived at the address shown in paragraph 2 above for at least 40 days immediately before I signed this application

7. DETAILS OF PRESENT MARRIAGE

Place of Marriage . . . .(Registration District)

Date of Marriage:(Day). . . . .(month). . . . .(year). . . . .

8. PERIOD OF SEPARATION

(i)   Please state the date on which you ceased to live with your spouse. (If more than 5 years, just give the month and year) Day. . . . . Month. . . . . Year. . . . .

(ii)   Have you lived with your spouse since that date?   *[YES/NO]

(iii) If yes, for how long in total did you live together before finally separating again?
                                                    . . . . .months

(*continued*)

9. RECONCILIATION

Is there any reasonable prospect of reconciliation with your
spouse?   *[YES/NO]

Do you consider that the marriage has broken down
irretrievably?   *[YES/NO]

10. MENTAL DISORDER

Is your spouse suffering from any mental disorder (whether
illness or handicap?) (If yes, give details)   *[YES/NO]

11. CHILDREN

Are there any children of the marriage under the age of 16? *[YES/NO]

12. OTHER COURT ACTIONS

Are you aware of any court actions currently
proceeding in any country (including Scotland) which
may affect your marriage?
(If yes, give details)   *[YES/NO]

*Delete as appropriate

13. DECLARATION AND REQUEST FOR DIVORCE

I confirm that the facts stated in paragraphs 1–11 above apply to my marriage.

I do NOT ask the sheriff to make any financial provision in connection with this
application.

I believe that no grave financial handship will be caused to my spouse as a result
of the granting of this application.

I request the sheriff to grant decree of divorce from my husband or wife.

Date ....
Signature of Applicant ....

PART 2

APPLICANT'S AFFIDAVIT

(To be completed by the Applicant only after Part 1 has been signed and dated.)

I, (*insert full name*).................................
residing at (*insert present home address*).............
....

212

SWEAR that to the best of my knowledge and belief that the facts stated in Part 1 of this Application are true.

Signature of Applicant..............................

To be completed by Justice of the Peace, Notary Public or Commissioner for Oaths	SWORN at (*insert place*)........................... this.............day of.............19............ before me (*insert full name*)....................... of (*insert full address*)........................... .... Signature....................................... *Justice of the Peace/Notary Public/Commissioner for Oaths

*Delete as appropriate

FORM F34   Rule 33.76(3)(a)

Form of citation in application relying on the facts in section 1(2)(d) of the Divorce (Scotland) Act 1976

(*Insert name and address of non-applicant spouse*)

APPLICATION FOR DIVORCE (HUSBAND AND WIFE HAVING LIVED APART FOR AT LEAST TWO YEARS WITH CONSENT OF OTHER PARTY)

Your spouse has applied to the sheriff for divorce on the ground that the marriage has broken down irretrievably because you and he or she have lived apart for a period of at least two years and you consent to divorce being granted.

A copy of the application is hereby served upon you.

1. Please note:
   (a) that the sheriff may not make financial provision under this procedure and that your spouse is making no claim for –
   (i) the payment by you of a periodical allowance (i.e. a regular payment of money weekly or monthly, etc. for maintenance);
   (ii) the payment by you of a capital sum (i.e. a lump sum payment);
   (b) that your spouse states that you will not suffer grave financial hardship in the event of decree of divorce being granted.
2. Divorce may result in the loss to you of property rights (e.g. the right to succeed to the Applicant's estate on his or her death) or the right, where appropriate, to a widow's pension.
3. If you wish to oppose the granting of a divorce, you should put your reasons in writing and send your letter to the address shown below. Your letter must reach the sheriff clerk before (*insert date*).

(*continued*)

4. In the event of the divorce being granted, you will be sent a copy of the extract decree. Should you change your address before receiving the copy extract decree, please notify the sheriff clerk immediately.

Signed
Sheriff clerk (depute)
(*insert address and telephone
number of the sheriff court*)
or Sheriff Officer

NOTE: If you wish to exercise your right to make a claim for financial provision you should immediately advise the sheriff clerk that you oppose the application for that reason, and thereafter consult a solicitor.

FORM F35   Rule 33.76(3)(b)

Form of citation in application relying on the facts in section 1(2)(e) of the Divorce (Scotland) Act 1976

(*Insert name and address of non-applicant spouse*)

APPLICATION FOR DIVORCE (HUSBAND AND WIFE HAVING LIVED APART FOR AT LEAST FIVE YEARS)

Your spouse has applied to the sheriff for divorce on the ground that the marriage has broken down irretrievably because you and he or she have lived apart for a period of at least five years.

A copy of the application is hereby served upon you.

1. Please note:
   (a) that the sheriff may not make financial provision under this procedure and that your spouse is making no claim for −
   (i) the payment by you of a periodical allowance (i.e. a regular payment of money weekly or monthly, etc. for maintenance);
   (ii) the payment by you of a capital sum (i.e. a lump sum payment);
   (b) that your spouse states that you will not suffer grave financial hardship in the event of decree of divorce being granted.
2. Divorce may result in the loss to you of property rights (e.g. the right to succeed to the Applicant's estate on his or her death) or the right, where appropriate, to a widow's pension.
3. If you wish to oppose the granting of a divorce, you should put your reasons in writing and send your letter to the address shown below. Your letter must reach the sheriff clerk before (*insert date*).

4. In the event of the divorce being granted, you will be sent a copy of the extract decree. Should you change your address before receiving the copy extract decree, please notify the sheriff clerk immediately.

Signed

Sheriff clerk (depute) (*insert
the address and
telephone number of the
sheriff court*)
or Sheriff officer

NOTE: If you wish to exercise your right to make a claim for financial provision you should immediately advise the sheriff clerk that you oppose the application for that reason, and thereafter consult a solicitor.

FORM F36 Rule 33.77(1)(a)

**Form of intimation of simplified divorce application for display on the
walls of court**

Court ref.no.

An application for divorce has been made in this sheriff court by
[A.B.], (*insert designation and address*), Applicant, naming [C.D.], (*insert
designation and address*) as Respondent.

If [C.D.], wishes to oppose the granting of decree of divorce he [*or* she] should immediately contact the sheriff clerk from whom he [*or* she] may obtain a copy of the application.

Date (*insert date*) Signed

Sheriff clerk (depute)

FORM F37 Rule 33.77(2)

Form of intimation to children and next-of-kin in simplified divorce application

To (*insert name and address*) Court ref.no.

You are hereby given NOTICE that an application for divorce has been made against (*insert name of respondent*) your (*insert relationship e.g. father, mother,
brother or other relative as the case may be*). A copy of this application is attached.

(*continued*)

215

Appendix 1

If you know of his or her present address, you are requested to inform the sheriff clerk (*insert address of sheriff clerk*) in writing immediately. You may also, if you wish, oppose the granting of decree of divorce by sending a letter to the court giving your reasons for your opposition to the application. Your letter must be sent to the sheriff clerk within 21 days of (*insert date on which intimation was given. N.B. Rule 5.3(2) relating to postal service or intimation*).

Date (*insert date*)   Signed

                                    Sheriff clerk (depute)

NOTE
IF YOU ARE UNCERTAIN WHAT ACTION TO TAKE you should consult a solicitor. You may be entitled to legal aid depending on your financial circumstances, and you can get information about legal aid from a solicitor. You may also obtain advice from any Citizens Advice Bureau or other advice agency.

FORM F38   Rule 33.80(2)

Form of extract decree of divorce in simplified divorce application

At (*insert place and date*)

in an action in the Sheriff Court of the Sheriffdom of (*insert name of sheriffdom*) at (*insert place of sheriff court*)

at the instance of [A.B.], (*insert full name of applicant*), Applicant,

against (*insert full name of respondent*), Respondent,

who were married at (*insert place*) on (*insert date*),

the sheriff pronounced decree divorcing the Respondent from the Applicant.

Extracted at (*insert place and date*)

by me, sheriff clerk of the Sheriffdom of (*insert name of sheriffdom*).

                                    Signed

                                    Sheriff clerk (depute)

FORM F39   Rule 33.90

**Form of certificate relating to the making of a maintenance assessment
under the Child Support Act 1991**

Sheriff Court (*insert address*)
Date (*insert date*)

I certify that notification has been received from the Secretary of State under
section 10 of the Child Support Act 1991 of the making of a maintenance
assessment under that Act which supersedes the decree or order granted on (*insert
date*) in relation to aliment for (*insert the name(s) of child(ren)*) with effect from
(*insert date*).

Signed
Sheriff clerk (depute)

FORM F40   Rule 33.90

**Form of certificate relating to the cancellation or ceasing to have effect of a
maintenance assessment under the Child Support Act 1991**

Sheriff Court (*insert address*)
Date (*insert date*)

I certify that notification has been received from the Secretary of State under
section 10 of the Child Support Act 1991 that the maintenance assessment made
on (*insert date*) has been cancelled [*or* ceased to have effect] on (*insert date*).

Signed
Sheriff clerk (depute)

FORM H1   Rule 34.1(2)

**Form of notice informing defender of right to apply for certain orders
under the Debtors (Scotland) Act 1987 on sequestration for rent**

Sheriff Court (*insert address*)   Court ref.no.

You are given NOTICE that, where articles are sequestrated for rent you have the
right to apply to the sheriff for certain orders under the Debtors (Scotland) Act
1987.

1. You may apply to the sheriff within fourteen days after the date the articles are
sequestrated for an order releasing any article on the ground that:
    (a) it is exempt from sequestration for rent (articles which are exempt are listed
    in section 16 of the Debtors (Scotland) Act 1987); or

(b) its inclusion in the sequestration for rent or its subsequent sale is unduly harsh.

2. Where a mobile home, such as a caravan, is your only or principal residence and it has been sequestrated for rent you may apply to the sheriff before a warrant to sell is granted for an order that for a specified period no further steps shall be taken in the sequestration.

Any enquiry relating to the above rights should be made to a solicitor, Citizens Advice Bureau or other advice centre or to the sheriff clerk at the above address.

FORM H2   Rule 34.6(1)

Form of notice of removal

To (*insert name, designation, and address of party in possession*). You are required to remove from (*describe subjects*) at the term of (*or if different terms, state them and the subjects to which they apply*), in terms of lease (*describe it*) [*or* in terms of your letter of removal dated (*insert date*)] [*or otherwise as the case may be*].

Date (*insert date*)   Signed

                           (*add designation and address*)

FORM H3   Rule 34.6(2)

Form of letter of removal

To (*insert name and designation of addressee*)
(*Insert place and date*) I am to remove from (*state subjects by usual name or short description sufficient for identification*) at the term of (*insert term and date*)

                [K.L.] (*add designation and address*).

(*If not holograph, to be attested thus* –

                [M.N.] (*add designation and address*), witness).

FORM H4   Rule 34.7

Form of notice of removal under section 37 of the 1907 Act

NOTICE OF REMOVAL UNDER SECTION 37 OF THE SHERIFF COURTS (SCOTLAND) ACT 1907

To (*insert designation and address*).
You are required to remove from (*insert description of heritable subjects, land, ground etc.*) at the term of [Whitsunday or Martinmas], (*insert date*)
Date (*insert date*)   Signed
                                                (*add designation and address*)

FORM M1   Rule 35.5

Form of warrant of citation in an action of multiplepoinding

(*Insert place and date*) Grants warrant to cite the defender (*insert name and address*) by serving a copy of the writ and warrant upon a period of notice of (*insert period of notice*) days, and ordains him [*or* her], if he [*or* she] intends to lodge:-
(a) defences challenging the jurisdiction of the court or the competence of the action; or
(b) objections to the condescendence on the fund *in medio*; or
(c) a claim on the fund;
to lodge a notice of appearance with the sheriff clerk at (*insert name and address of sheriff court*) within the said period of notice after such service [and grants warrant to arrest on the dependence].

[*Where the holder of the fund in medio is a defender, insert*: Appoints the holder of the fund *in medio* to
(a) lodge with the sheriff clerk at (*insert place of sheriff court*) within the said period of notice after such service
    (i) a detailed condescendence on the fund *in medio*; and
    (ii) a list of parties having an interest in the fund; and
(b) intimate to all parties to the action a copy of the condescendence and list.]

FORM M2   Rule 35.6(1)

Form of citation in an action of multiplepoinding

CITATION

SHERIFFDOM OF (*insert name of sheriffdom*)   Court ref.no.
AT (*insert place of sheriff court*)

[A.B.], (*insert designation and address*), Pursuer against [C.D.], (*insert designation and address*) Defender

                                                (*continued*)

(*Insert place and date*) You [C.D.] are hereby served with this copy writ and warrant, together with Form M4 (notice of appearance).

[*Where the defender is the holder of the fund in medio, insert the following paragraph:-*
As holder of the fund *in medio* you must lodge with the sheriff clerk at the above address within (*insert period of notice*)   days of (*insert date on which service was executed. N.B. Rule 5.3(2) relating to postal service*) –
(a) a detailed condescendence on the fund *in medio*; and
(b) a list of parties having an interest in the fund.
You must at the same time intimate to all other parties to the action a copy of
(a) the detailed condescendence on the fund; and
(b) the list of parties having an interest in the fund.]

Form M4 is served on you for use should you wish to intimate that you intend to lodge:-

(a) defences challenging the jurisdiction of the court or the competence of the action; or
(b) objections to the condescendence on the fund *in medio*; or
(c) a claim on the fund.

IF YOU WISH TO APPEAR IN THIS ACTION you should consult a solicitor with a view to lodging a notice of appearance (Form M4). The notice of appearance, together with the court fee of £(*insert amount*) must be lodged with the sheriff clerk at the above address within (*insert the appropriate period of notice*)   days of (*insert the date on which service was executed. N.B. Rule 5.3(2) relating to postal service*).

IF YOU ARE UNCERTAIN WHAT ACTION TO TAKE you should consult a solicitor. You may be eligible for legal aid depending on your income. You can get information about legal aid from a solicitor. You may also obtain advice from any Citizens Advice Bureau or other advice agency.

PLEASE NOTE THAT IF YOU DO NOTHING IN ANSWER TO THIS DOCUMENT the court may regard you as having no interest in the fund *in medio* and will proceed accordingly.

Signed
      [P.Q.], Sheriff officer,
      or [X.Y.] (*add designation and business address*)
      Solicitor for the pursuer

Form M3 Rule 35.6(2)

Form of certificate of citation in an action of multiplepoinding

CERTIFICATE OF CITATION

(*Insert place and date*) I, hereby certify that upon the day of

I duly cited [C.D.], Defender, to answer to the foregoing writ. This I did by (*state method of service; if by officer and not by post, add:* in presence of [L.M.], (*insert designation*), witness hereto with me subscribing; *and where service is executed by post state whether made by registered post or the first class recorded delivery service*).

Signed
[P.Q.], Sheriff officer
[L.M.], witness
or [X.Y.], (*add designation and business address*)
Solicitor for the pursuer

FORM M4 Rule 35.6(1) and 35.8

Form of notice of appearance in an action of multiplepoinding

*Part A **NOTICE OF APPEARANCE (MULTIPLEPOINDING)**
Court ref.no.

in an action raised at Sheriff Court

(*Insert name and business address of solicitor for the pursuer*)

Pursuer

Solicitor for the pursuer

Defender

*(This part to be completed by the pursuer before service)

DATE OF SERVICE: DATE OF EXPIRY OF PERIOD OF NOTICE:
....

(*continued*)

Appendix 1

*PART B

*(This section to be completed by the defender or the defender's solicitor and both parts of this form returned to the sheriff clerk at (*insert address of sheriff clerk*) on or before the expiry of the period of notice referred to in PART A above)

(*Insert place and date*)
[C.D.] (*design*), Defender, intends to lodge:

Tick the appropriate box(es)

☐ defences challenging the jurisdiction of the court or the competence of the action.

☐ objections to the condescendence on the fund *in medio*

☐ a claim on the fund *in medio*.

Signed
[C.D.] Defender,
or [X.Y.] (*add designation and business address*) Solicitor for the defender

Form M5   Rules 35.9(b) and 35.10(5)

Form of intimation of first hearing in an action of multiplepoinding

SHERIFFDOM OF (*insert name of sheriffdom*)   Court ref.no.
AT (*insert place of sheriff court*)

[A.B.] (*insert designation and address*), Pursuer, against, [C.D.] (*insert designation and address*), Defender

You are given notice that in this action of multiplepoinding

(*Insert date, time and place*)   is the date, time and place for the first hearing.

Date (*insert date*)   Signed
                              Sheriff clerk (depute)

222

NOTE

If the pursuer fails to return the writ in terms of rule 9.3 of the Ordinary Cause Rules of the Sheriff Court or any party fails to comply with the terms of this notice or to provide the sheriff at the hearing with sufficient information to enable it to be conducted in terms of rule 35.10 of these Rules, the sheriff may make such order or finding against that party so failing as he thinks fit.

NOTE TO BE ADDED WHERE PARTY UNREPRESENTED

NOTE

IF YOU ARE UNCERTAIN WHAT ACTION TO TAKE you should consult a solicitor. You may be eligible for legal aid depending on your income. You can get information about legal aid from a solicitor. You may also obtain advice from any Citizens Advice Bureau or other advice agency.

Form M6 Rule 35.10(4)(b)

Form of citation of person having an interest in the fund in an action of multiplepoinding

CITATION

SHERIFFDOM OF (*insert name of sheriffdom*) Court ref.no.
AT (*insert place of sheriff court*)

[A.B.], (*insert designation and address*), Pursuer, against [C.D.], (*insert designation and address*), Defender

(*Insert place and date*) In the above action the court has been advised that you (*insert name and address*) have an interest in (*insert details of the fund in medio*). You are hereby served with a copy of the pleadings in this action, together with Form M4 (notice of appearance).

Form M4 is served on you for use should you wish to intimate that you intend to lodge:-

(a) defences challenging the jurisdiction of the court or the competence of the action; or
(b) objections to the condescendence on the fund *in medio*; or
(c) a claim on the fund.

(*continued*)

IF YOU WISH TO APPEAR IN THIS ACTION you should consult a solicitor with a view to lodging a notice of appearance (Form M4). The notice of appearance, together with the court fee of £ (*insert amount*) must be lodged with the sheriff clerk at the above address within   days of (*insert date on which service was executed. N.B. Rule 5.3(2) relating to postal service*).

NOTE

IF YOU ARE UNCERTAIN WHAT ACTION TO TAKE you should consult a solicitor. You may be eligible for legal aid depending on your income. You can get information about legal aid from a solicitor. You may also obtain advice from any Citizens Advice Bureau or other advice agency.

PLEASE NOTE THAT IF YOU DO NOTHING IN ANSWER TO THIS DOCUMENT the court may regard you as having no interest in the fund *in medio* and will proceed accordingly.

Signed
[P.Q.], Sheriff officer,
or [X.Y.] (*add designation and business address*)
Solicitor for the pursuer

Form D1   Rule 36.3(2)

Form of intimation to connected person in damages action

SHERIFFDOM OF (*insert name of sheriffdom*)   Court ref.no.
AT (*insert place of sheriff court*)

You are given NOTICE that an action has been raised in the above sheriff court by (*insert name and designation of pursuer*) against (*insert name and designation of defender*).
A copy of the initial writ is attached.

It is believed that you may have a title or interest to sue the said (*insert name of defender*) in an action based upon [the injuries from which the late (*insert name and designation*) died] [*or* the death of the late (*insert name and designation*)]. You may therefore be entitled to enter this action as an additional pursuer. If you wish to do so, you may apply by lodging a minute with the sheriff clerk at the above address to be sisted as an additional pursuer within (*insert the appropriate period of notice*) days of (*insert the date on which service was executed. N.B. Rule 5.3(2) relating to postal service*).

Signed
Solicitor for the pursuer

NOTE
The minute must be lodged with the sheriff clerk with the court fee of (*insert amount*) and a motion seeking leave for the minute to be received and for answers to be lodged. When lodging the minute you must present to the sheriff clerk a copy of the initial writ and this intimation.

IF YOU ARE UNCERTAIN WHAT ACTION TO TAKE you should consult a solicitor. You may be eligible for legal aid depending on your income, and you can obtain information about legal aid from any solicitor. You may also obtain advice from any Citizens Advice Bureau or other advice agency.

FORM D2 Rule 36.17(1)

Form of receipt for payment into court

RECEIPT

In the Sheriff Court of (*insert name of sheriffdom*) at (*insert place of sheriff court*) in the cause, (*state names of parties or other appropriate description*) [A.B.] (*insert designation*) has this day paid into court the sum of (*insert sum concerned*) being a payment into court in terms of rule 36.14 of the Ordinary Cause Rules of the Sheriff Court of money which in an action of damages, has become payable to a person under legal disability.

[*If the payment is made under rule 36.15(c) add:* [the custody of which money has been accepted at the request of (*insert name of court making request*).]

Date (*insert date*)   Signed
                                         Sheriff clerk (depute)

FORM P1 Rule 37.2(2)

**Form of advertisement in an action of declarator under section 1(1)
of the Presumption of Death (Scotland) Act 1977**

Sheriff Court (*insert address*)   Court ref.no.

An action has been raised in (*insert name of sheriff court*) by [A.B.], Pursuer, to declare that [C.D.], Defender, whose last known address was (*insert last known address of* [C.D.]) is dead. Any person wishing to defend the action must apply to do so by (*insert date, being* [*21*] *days after the date of the advertisement*) by lodging a minute seeking to be sisted as a party to the action with the sheriff clerk at the above address.

(*continued*)

225

Appendix 1

A copy of the initial writ may be obtained from the sheriff clerk at the above address.

Date (*insert date*)   Signed
                              [X.Y.] (*add designation and business address*) Solicitor for the pursuer or [P.Q.] Sheriff Officer

Form P2   Rule 37.2(4)

Form of intimation to missing person's spouse and children or nearest known relative

To (*insert name and address as in warrant*)   Court ref.no.

You are given notice that in this action the pursuer craves the court to declare that (*insert the name and last known address of missing person*) is dead. A copy of the initial writ is enclosed.

If you wish to appear as a party, and make an application under section 1(5) of the Presumption of Death (Scotland) Act 1977 craving the court to make any determintion or appointment not sought by the pursuer, you must lodge a minute with the sheriff clerk at (*insert address of sheriff clerk*).
Your minute must be lodged within [   ] days of (*insert the date on which intimation was given. N.B. Rule 5.3(2) relating to postal service or intimation*).

Date (*insert date*)   Signed
                              Solicitor for the pursuer
                              (*add designation and business address*)

NOTE
If you decide to lodge a minute it may be in your best interest to consult a solicitor. The minute should be lodged with the sheriff clerk with the appropriate fee of £ (*insert amount*) and a copy of this intimation.

IF YOU ARE UNCERTAIN WHAT ACTION TO TAKE you should consult a solicitor. You may be entitled to legal aid depending on your financial circumstances. You can get information about legal aid from a solicitor. You may also obtain advice from any Citizens Advice Bureau or other advice agency.

FORM E1   RULE 38.2(2)

**Form of request for preliminary ruling of the Court of Justice of the
European Communities**

SHERIFFDOM OF (*insert name of sheriffdom*)   Court ref.no.
AT (*insert place of court*)
in the cause
[A.B.], (*insert designation and address*), Pursuer
against
[C.D.], (*insert designation and address*), Defender

(*Here set out a statement of the case for the European Court, giving brief
particulars of the case and issues between the parties, and relevant facts found by
the court, any relevant rules and provisions of Scots Law, and the relevant Treaty
provisions, acts, instruments or rules of Community Law giving rise to the
reference*).

The preliminary ruling of the Court of Justice of the European Communities is
accordingly sought on the following questions (*insert in numerical sequence the
questions on which the ruling is sought*):

Date (*insert date*)   Signed
                                          Sheriff (*insert designation*)

Appendix 2

Forms for Extract Decrees

FORM 1

Form of extract decree for payment

EXTRACT DECREE   FOR PAYMENT

Sheriff Court   Court ref.no.

Date of decree   *In absence

Pursuer(s)   Defender(s)

The sheriff granted decree against the   for payment to the
of the undernoted sums.

Sum decerned for £   with interest at   per cent a year from   until
payment and expenses against the   of £   .

*A time to pay direction was made under section 1(1) of the Debtors (Scotland)
Act 1987.

*The amount is payable by instalments of £   per
commencing within   of intimation of this extract decree.

*The amount is payable by lump sum within   of intimation of this extract
decree.

This extract is warrant for all lawful execution hereon.

Date   Sheriff clerk (depute)

*Delete as appropriate.

228

FORM 2

Form of extract decree ad factum praestandum

EXTRACT DECREE *AD FACTUM PRAESTANDUM*

Sheriff Court   Court ref.no.

Date of decree   *In absence

Pursuer(s)   Defender(s)

The sheriff ordained the defender(s)

and granted decree against the   for payment of expenses of £

This extract is warrant for all lawful execution hereon.

Date   Sheriff clerk (depute)

*Delete as appropriate.

Appendix 2

FORM 3

Form of extract decree of removing

EXTRACT DECREE OF REMOVING

Sheriff Court   Court ref.no.

Date of decree   *In absence

Pursuer(s)   Defender(s)

The sheriff ordained the defender(s) to remove *himself/herself/themselves *and* his/her/their sub-tenants, dependents and others, and all effects from the premises at the undernoted address and to leave those premises vacant ** [and that after a charge of   days].

In the event that the defender(s) fail(s) to remove the sheriff granted warrant to sheriff officers to eject the defender(s), sub-tenants, dependents and others, with all effects, from those premises so as to leave them vacant.

The sheriff granted decree against the   for payment of expenses of £   .

Full address of premises:-

This extract is warrant for all lawful execution hereon.

Date   Sheriff clerk (depute)

*Delete as appropriate.
**Delete if period of charge is not specified in the decree.

FORM 4

Form of extract decree of declarator

EXTRACT DECREE OF DECLARATOR

Sheriff Court   Court ref.no.

Date of decree   *In absence

Pursuer(s)   Defender(s)

The sheriff found and declared that

and granted decree against the   for payment of expenses of £

This extract is warrant for all lawful execution hereon.

Date   Sheriff clerk (depute)

*Delete as appropriate.

FORM 5

Form of extract decree of furthcoming

EXTRACT DECREE OF FURTHCOMING

Sheriff Court   Court ref.no.

Date of decree   *In absence

Date of original decree

Pursuer(s)   Defender(s)/Arrestee(s)

Common Debtor(s)

The sheriff granted decree against the arrestee(s) for payment of the undernoted sums.

Sum decerned for £   or such other sum(s) as may be owing by the arrestee(s) to the common debtor(s) by virtue of the original decree dated above in favour of the pursuer(s) against the common debtor(s).

Expenses of £   *payable out of the arrested fund/payable by the common debtor(s).

This extract is warrant for all lawful execution hereon.

Date   Sheriff clerk (depute)

*Delete as appropriate.

FORM 6

Form of extract decree of absolvitor

EXTRACT DECREE OF ABSOLVITOR

Sheriff Court

Court ref.no.

Date of first warrant

Date of decree

Pursuer(s)

Defender(s)

(*Insert the nature of crave(s) in the above action*)

The sheriff absolved the   defender(s)
and granted decree against the   for payment of expenses of £   .

This extract is warrant for all lawful execution hereon.

Date

Sheriff clerk (depute)

FORM 7

Form of extract decree of dismissal

EXTRACT DECREE OF DISMISSAL

Sheriff Court   Court ref.no.

Date of first warrant   Date of decree

Pursuer(s)   Defender(s)

The sheriff dismissed the action against the   defender(s)
and granted decree against the   for payment of expenses of £   .

*This extract is warrant for all lawful execution hereon.

Date   Sheriff clerk (depute)

*Delete as appropriate.

FORM 8

**Form of extract decree under the Conveyancing and Feudal Reform
(Scotland) Act 1970**

EXTRACT DECREE UNDER THE CONVEYANCING AND FEUDAL
REFORM (SCOTLAND) ACT 1970

Sheriff Court   Court ref.no.

Date of decree   *In absence

Pursuer(s)   Defender(s)

The sheriff granted warrant to the pursuer(s) to enter into possession of the
subjects situated at the undernoted address and to exercise in relation to those
subjects all of the remedies competent to a creditor in lawful possession of the
subjects, by virtue of the Conveyancing and Feudal Reform (Scotland) Act 1970,
and in particular granted warrant to the pursuer(s) to sell those subjects.

The sheriff ordained the defender(s) to remove *himself/herself/themselves *and*
his/her/their sub-tenants, dependents and others and all effects from the subjects
and to leave them vacant.

In the event that the defender(s) fail(s) to remove the sheriff granted warrant to
sheriff officers to eject the defender(s), sub-tenants, dependents and others, with
all effects, from the subjects so as to leave them vacant.

The sheriff granted decree against the   for payment of expenses of £   .

Full address of subjects:-

This extract is warrant for all lawful execution hereon.

Date   Sheriff clerk (depute)

*Delete as appropriate.

Appendix 2

Form of general extract decree

EXTRACT DECREE

Sheriff Court   Court ref.no.

Date of decree   *In absence

Pursuer(s)   Defender(s)

The sheriff

and granted decree against the   for payment of expenses of £   .

This extract is warrant for all lawful execution hereon.

Date   Sheriff clerk (depute)

*Delete as appropriate.

236

FORM 10

Form of extract decree of divorce

EXTRACT DECREE OF DIVORCE

Sheriff Court	Court ref.no.
Date of decree	*In absence
Pursuer	Defender

Date of parties marriage	Place of parties marriage

The sheriff granted decree

(1) divorcing the defender from the pursuer;

*(2) awarding custody to the *pursuer/defender of the following child(ren):

Full name(s)   Date(s) of birth

and finding the *pursuer/defender entitled to access to the following child(ren):

as follows:

*(3) ordaining payment

    *(a) by the   to the   of a periodical allowance of £   per   ;
    *(b) by the   to the   of a capital sum of £   ;
    *(c) by the   to the   of £   per   as aliment for each
        child until that child attains   years of age, said sum payable in advance
        and beginning at the date of this decree with interest thereon at the
        rate of   per cent a year until payment;
    *(d) by the   to the   of £   of expenses;

*(4) finding the   liable to the   in expenses as the same may be subsequently
    taxed.

This extract is warrant for all lawful execution hereon.

Date   Sheriff clerk (depute)

*Delete as appropriate.

FORM 11

Form of extract decree of separation and aliment

EXTRACT DECREE OF SEPARATION AND ALIMENT

Sheriff Court   Court ref.no.

Date of decree   *In absence

Pursuer   Defender

The sheriff found and declared that the pursuer is entitled to live separately from the defender from the date of decree and for all time thereafter.

The sheriff awarded custody to the *pursuer/defender of the following child(ren):

Full name(s)   Date(s) of birth

and found the *pursuer/defender entitled to access to the following child(ren): as follows:

*The sheriff ordained payment by the   to the   of £   per as aliment for the   , said sum payable in advance and beginning at the date of this decree with interest thereon at   per cent a year until payment.

*The sheriff ordained payment by the   to the   of £   per as aliment for each child, until that child attains   years of age, said sum payable in advance and beginning at the date of this decree with interest thereon at   per cent a year until payment;

and granted decree against the   for payment of expenses of £   .

This extract is warrant for all lawful execution hereon.

Date   Sheriff clerk (depute)

*Delete as appropriate.

FORM 12

Form of extract decree of custody and aliment

EXTRACT DECREE OF CUSTODY AND ALIMENT

Sheriff Court   Court ref.no.

Date of decree   *In absence

Pursuer   Defender

The sheriff granted decree against the *pursuer/defender.

The sheriff awarded custody to the *pursuer/defender of the following child(ren):

Full name(s)   Date(s) of birth

and found the *pursuer/defender entitled to access to the following child(ren): as follows:

The sheriff ordained payment by the   to the   of £   per   as aliment for each child, until that child attains   years of age, said sum payable in advance and beginning at the date of this decree with interest thereon at   per cent a year until payment;

and granted decree against the   for payment of expenses of £   .

This extract is warrant for all lawful execution hereon.

Date   Sheriff clerk (depute)

*Delete as appropriate.

FORM 13

Form of extract decree of affiliation and aliment

EXTRACT DECREE OF AFFILIATION AND ALIMENT

Sheriff Court   Court ref.no.

Date of Decree   *In absence

Pursuer   Defender

The sheriff, in respect that the defender is the father of the child named below, granted decree against the defender for the sum(s) undernoted.

Full name of child

Date of birth   Place of birth

Registration district   Birth entry no.

Aliment of £   per   commencing on

Inlying expenses of £   .   Interest at   per cent a year from

       until payment and expenses, against the   of £   .

       This extract is warrant for all lawful execution hereon.

Date   Sheriff clerk (depute)

*Delete as appropriate.

Index

Index